BLACK AMERICAN

GREAT AMBITIONS

BA

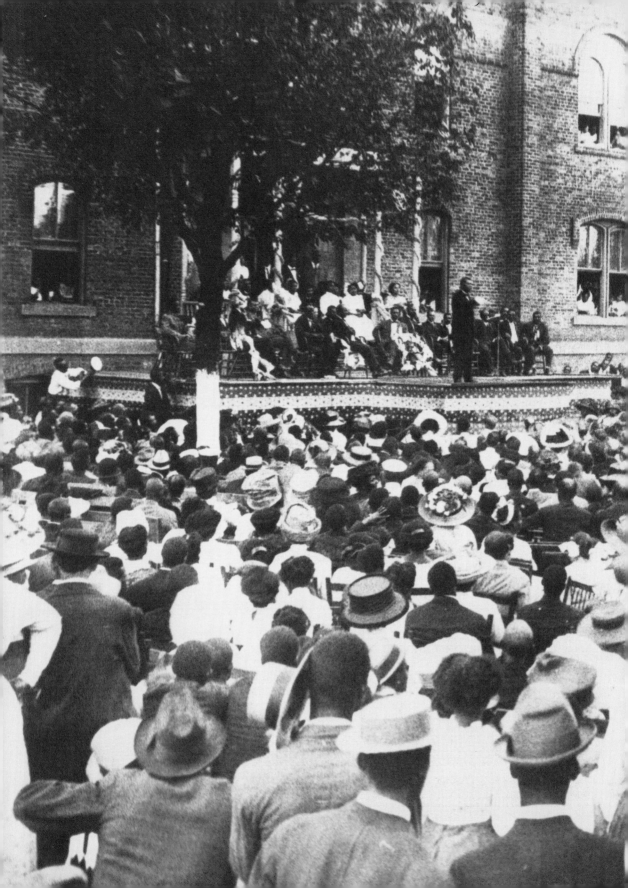

GREAT AMBITIONS

FROM THE "SEPARATE BUT EQUAL" DOCTRINE TO THE BIRTH OF THE NAACP (1896-1909)

Pierre Hauser

CHELSEA HOUSE PUBLISHERS
New York   Philadelphia

FRONTISPIECE Booker T. Washington addresses a spellbound audience at Tuskegee Institute, the celebrated school he established in Tuskegee, Alabama, in 1881.

ON THE COVER Founding members of the Niagara Movement, America's first major civil rights organization, gather for their original meeting, held near Niagara Falls, Canada, in July 1905. W. E. B. Du Bois, the moving force of the new body, is in the center row, second from the right.

Chelsea House Publishers
Editorial Director Richard Rennert
Executive Managing Editor Karyn Gullen Browne
Copy Chief Robin James
Picture Editor Adrian G. Allen
Art Director Robert Mitchell
Manufacturing Director Gerald Levine
Assistant Art Director Joan Ferrigno

Milestones in Black American History
Senior Editor Marian W. Taylor
Series Originator and Adviser Benjamin I. Cohen
Series Consultants Clayborne Carson, Darlene Clark Hine
Series Designer Rae Grant

Staff for GREAT AMBITIONS
Editorial Assistants Sydra Mallery, Anne McDonnell
Picture Researcher Pat Burns

Copyright © 1995 by Chelsea House Publishers, a division of Main Line Book Co. All rights reserved. Printed and bound in the United States of America.

First Printing

1 3 5 7 9 8 6 4 2

Library of Congress Cataloging-in-Publication Data

Hauser, Pierre (Pierre N.)
   Great Ambitions, 1896–1909: from the "separate but equal" doctrine to the birth of the NAACP/Pierre Hauser.
       p. cm. — (Milestones in Black American history)
   Includes bibliographical references and index.
       ISBN 0-7910-2264-1
       ISBN 0-7910-2690-6 (pbk.)
   1.Civil rights movements—United States—History—Juvenile literature. 2.Afro-Americans—Civil rights—Juvenile literature. 3.Afro-Americans—Segregation—Ju-venile literature. 4. Southern States—Race relations—Juvenile literature. [1.Civil rights movements—History. 2.Afro-Americans—Civil rights. 3. Southern States—Race relations.] I. Title. II. Series.
E185.61.H385 1995   94-21875
323.1'196073'009034—dc20   CIP
                                                                             AC

CONTENTS

MILESTONES IN BLACK AMERICAN HISTORY

INTRODUCTION

In early youth a great bitterness entered my life and kindled a great ambition. I wanted to go to college because others did. I came and graduated and... am now in search of bread. I believe, foolishly perhaps but sincerely, that I have something to say to the world.

—W.E.B. Du Bois

W hen the Civil War ended in 1865, African Americans headed straight for full citizenship—until they were stopped in their tracks in 1896. Blocking their way was *Plessy v. Ferguson*, the notorious U.S. Supreme Court ruling that made racial segregation the law of the land. Once bright with promise, the years between 1896 and 1909 were to provide blacks with their darkest hours since slavery.

Plessy enshrined a practice that was clearly meant to humiliate, stigmatize, and isolate blacks. From 1896 on, any community could legally separate the races in any public place, from schools to trains to cemeteries. In law, such segregation was entirely acceptable as long as the facilities offered to each race were "equal." But in reality, blacks— especially in the South—were almost never offered the same quality of services as whites. (Black public schools, for example, received about a quarter of the funds allotted to white schools.)

Immediately after the Civil War, Congress passed specific acts to protect blacks and to help them embark on their new lives. *Plessy* brought that era to a close. From 1896 on, the court seemed to be saying, the U.S. government would no longer act to guarantee the rights of African Americans.

During the years after *Plessy*, state and local governments in the South, where 90 percent of blacks then lived, greatly expanded the reach of segregation. Before the ruling, most racial division had occurred in education and transportation; afterward, it was extended into almost every area of life. New laws segregated parks, restaurants, factories, public restrooms, water fountains, residential areas, sports— virtually every place where people came together in public.

Meanwhile, southern white supremacists acted to deprive blacks of their constitutional right to vote. Before 1896, only two southern states had enacted laws disfranchising blacks. Between 1896 and 1903, four states amended their constitutions to create poll taxes, literacy tests, and property requirements that effectively kept most black citizens from voting. The rest of the former Confederate states established similar restrictions on black voting. In Louisiana alone, the number of blacks registered to vote dropped from 130,000 in 1898 to 5,000 in 1902.

Southern whites discouraged blacks from rebelling against this system of racial oppression—known as Jim Crow—by using savage violence: in a crime called lynching, vigilante mobs periodically murdered blacks who challenged the color line. (The term Jim Crow first became a derogatory name for African Americans with the popularity of a music-hall dance in which white performers in black-face makeup would sing, "Jump, Jim Crow" while performing a ridiculous jumping dance.) In addition to lynchings, whites resorted to large-scale attacks on black communities. In 1898, whites in Wilmington, North Carolina, accused blacks of thwarting the election of Populist party candidates; to punish them, mobs of armed whites burned and slashed their way through the town's black neighborhoods. In 1906, white gangs in Atlanta, Georgia, killed 12 blacks and destroyed scores of black-owned buildings in retaliation for four alleged rapes of white women; the rapes were later shown to be the product of a reporter's imagination. And in 1908, whites in Springfield, Illinois, sought to avenge another fictitious rape by assaulting hundreds of blacks. One of the victims was an 84-year-old man whose "crime" was his happy 30-year marriage to a white woman.

Aware that protesting against Jim Crow often triggered violence, most black leaders promoted accommodation, or giving in to whites. This was the approach of Booker T. Washington, head of Alabama's Tuskegee Institute and arguably the most powerful black man in America. Washington's willingness to compromise endeared him to southern whites, who mistakenly assumed that he accepted secondary status for blacks as a permanent condition. It also made him popular with northern whites, who believed his approach would help pave the way for the economic development of the South. Washington developed enormous influence with the white establishment; in 1896, for example, Harvard University awarded him an honorary degree—the first it had ever given an African American—and in 1901, President Theodore Roosevelt invited him to the White House.

Washington suppressed resistance to racial oppression, but he helped raise the quality of black lives in two important ways: he promoted the careers of black entrepreneurs through the National Negro Business League, which he founded in 1900, and he vastly improved black education by persuading John D. Rockefeller, Andrew Carnegie, and other northern industrialists to contribute millions of dollars to black schools, libraries, and colleges.

The years between 1896 and 1909—a time when few black leaders dared to press for change—were stained by some of the grimmest racism in American history. These same years, however, also revealed something of incalculable worth: the tremendous resilience of African Americans. For, amazingly enough, it was in this heyday of Jim Crow that the roots of the modern civil rights movement first took hold. Initially, only a few courageous individuals—most of them college-educated blacks in the North—raised their voices in protest.

Throughout the 1890s, journalist Ida Wells-Barnett conducted a ceaseless campaign against lynching, disseminating a flood of information about the murderous practice in lectures, articles, and books. In 1901, activist editor Monroe Trotter founded the *Guardian*, a Boston-based newspaper devoted to chronicling the evils of segregation and disfranchisement. And in 1903, Professor W. E. B. Du Bois made an eloquent case against Jim Crow in a book called *The Souls of Black Folk*. These individuals gradually came together as a united force.

In 1905, the first protest group, the Niagara Movement, was founded. This organization was weakened by its failure to attract support among whites and working-class blacks and by its use of mere words to fight racial prejudice. But in 1909, a second protest group, the National Association for the Advancement of Colored People (NAACP), came into being. This group did enlist the aid of white liberals and did discover potent methods—legal action in particular—for undermining the foundation of Jim Crow. So, by 1909, in spite of the hardening of racial oppression across the South, the first major civil rights group had been born. The NAACP would serve as the main civil rights organization for several decades, ultimately playing a major role in ending the South's race system.

Blacks made progress between 1896 and 1909 not only in fighting for their rights in relations with whites, but in developing their own institutions and communities. Black educational opportunities increased, especially in vocational instruction. Black businesses multiplied, notably in banking and insurance. Black mutual aid societies flourished, black churches strengthened their appeal through reforms and the provision of social services, black workers found new jobs in southern industry, black urban communities grew, a black middle class began to take form, and blacks explored new migratory routes to economic opportunities in the North.

African Americans also made large gains on the cultural front. Paul Laurence Dunbar and Charles Chesnutt emerged during the late 1890s as the first well-known black writers. Black painter Henry Ossawa Tanner's luminous religious canvases won awards across Europe and were collected by many prominent museums, including the Louvre in Paris. And black musicians such as Buddy Bolden, Scott Joplin and W. C. Handy introduced to America three important new musical forms: jazz, ragtime, and the blues.

The years between 1896 and 1909 were difficult and dispiriting for blacks. They were at the same time heartening and enlightening, thanks to the courage and genius of such political and cultural pioneers as Wells-Barnett, Du Bois, Chesnutt, and Joplin. Because of them and other remarkable people, the story of the turn-of-the-century black experience is not only a record of oppression and accommodation but one of protest and innovation.

MILESTONES
1896-1909

1896 • By a 7–1 vote, the U.S. Supreme Court rejects white attorney Albion W. Tourgée's argument that the constitutional rights of his black client, Homer A. Plessy, were violated when he was arrested for riding in a "whites-only" Louisiana train car. In the majority opinion of *Plessy v. Ferguson*, Justice Henry Billings Brown asserts that segregation is lawful as long as conditions are equal for both races. Until it is overturned in 1954, the *Plessy* decision will strengthen Jim Crow and encourage a wave of racist laws throughout the South.

• Between 1896 and 1906, blacks in nearly 30 southern cities boycott transportation companies that introduce segregated seating areas; in Nashville, Chattanooga, Savannah, and Houston, blacks form their own trolley services.

• Booker T. Washington, the former slave who became president of Tuskegee Institute, receives an honorary master's degree from Harvard University, the first such distinction accorded an African American.

• Washington appoints George Washington Carver to head an agricultural training program at Tuskegee; famous for his research on peanuts, Carver is soon recognized as the nation's most distinguished agricultural scientist.

• Editor and antilynching activist Ida Wells-Barnett cofounds the National Association of Colored Women. The organization's first president, Mary Church Terrell, speaks out against racial discrimination and forms alliances with white feminists.

• Paul Laurence Dunbar's second collection of poems, *Majors and Minors*, is heralded in *Harper's Weekly* by renowned white novelist and critic William Dean Howells. Dunbar, who took the revolutionary step of writing poetry in black dialect, begins to gain a wide readership among blacks and whites.

• W. E. B. Du Bois publishes his seminal dissertation, *Suppression of the Slave Trade*, thus beginning his lifelong scholarly exposure of the injustices committed against the black race.

1897 • President William McKinley considers Booker T. Washington for a cabinet post until Washington professes lack of interest. A year later,

11

Washington attracts great publicity for himself and Tuskegee when he persuades McKinley to visit the institute.

- Henry Ossawa Tanner's luminous religious painting *Raising of Lazarus* is purchased by the French government after being much acclaimed at the Paris Salon des Artistes. Emerging as one of the most important artists— black or white—of the time, Tanner receives many honors.

1898

- The Supreme Court declares poll taxes and literacy tests constitutional; in the next few years, the Court expands this ruling to allow suffrage restrictions not explicitly based on race, color, or previous slave status.

- Louisiana introduces the South's first so-called grandfather clause, a regulation that gives the vote to any man whose grandfather had been qualified to vote in 1867. The requirements serve their purpose—to prevent blacks from voting. In Louisiana alone, the number of registered black voters plummets from 130,000 in 1898 to 5,000 in 1902.

- After losing the year's elections, white Populists blame their black allies and spark a vicious race riot in Wilmington, North Carolina; 20 blacks are killed. Subsequently, white Populists support Democrats in the institution of more Jim Crow laws.

- Wells-Barnett lobbies Congress for antilynching legislation and compensation for a lynching victim's family. President McKinley meets with her, but the Spanish-American War diverts attention from the issue.

- A number of blacks condemn the Spanish-American War—which results in U.S. acquisition of Puerto Rico, Guam, Cuba, and the Philippines—as an international extension of racism. However, many blacks join the war effort out of patriotism and loyalty to Republican president McKinley; two black units charge up San Juan Hill with Theodore Roosevelt's Rough Riders. After heroically rescuing 15 white soldiers, four black men from the 10th Cavalry are awarded the Congressional Medal of Honor, the country's highest decoration.

- Wells-Barnett revives the Afro-American League, a national organization for black unity, and steers it toward a radical course of agitation rather than accommodation. She is elected secretary of the league, which is renamed the Afro-American Council.

- Will Marion Cook's *Clorindy, the Origin of the Cakewalk*, the first Broadway show composed or directed by a black, exposes New York theatergoers to ragtime music and becomes a huge hit.

1899

- Washington hosts a benefit for Tuskegee Institute at New York City's

Madison Square Garden. The event draws major support from J. P. Morgan and John D. Rockefeller; Washington later elicits a $600,000 contribution to black education from white industrialist and philanthropist Andrew Carnegie.

- Wells-Barnett persuades the Afro-American Council to denounce Washington for comments that seemed to excuse several lynchings. In response, the National Association of Colored Women removes her from a leadership position.

- Charles Chesnutt publishes his first novel, *The Conjure Woman*. Though criticized for being too moderate in the face of racism, Chesnutt earns respect for his well-written, realistic depiction of black life. With gains in literacy, black writers find greater expression—by 1900, the nation boasts 150 black weekly newspapers, 3 black dailies, and 2 black magazines.

- Scott Joplin composes his first major ragtime work, "Maple Leaf Rag." (In 1976 Joplin will be awarded a posthumous Pulitzer Prize for his ground-breaking musical work.)

1900

- Washington founds the National Negro Business League to promote black enterprise. By 1911, the number of banks run by blacks has risen from 4 to 56.

- Washington publishes his classic autobiography *Up From Slavery*; by this time, Washington has developed such vast influence that his power base is sometimes called the "Tuskegee Machine."

- The black community's emphasis on education as a means of advancement reaps some results: 1.5 million black children attend school and 28,500 blacks are teachers—although only 700 blacks receive a college education. Enhanced education enables more blacks to take skilled jobs in urban areas, and a black middle class develops.

1901

- Theodore Roosevelt succeeds McKinley as president and makes Washington his unofficial chief adviser on black matters; to the horror of racists, Roosevelt entertains Washington at a White House dinner. Although unable to persuade the president to take action against lynching and black disfranchisement, Washington influences political appointments.

- William Monroe Trotter launches the *Guardian*, a black newspaper in Boston, to dispute Washington's policy of accommodation.

- Representative George White of North Carolina, the lone black in Congress, introduces legislation that would make lynching a federal offense. White's bill suffers defeat at the hands of southern Democrats and he loses office; he becomes the last black elected to Congress for 28 years.

1902
- Every former Confederate state has now introduced poll taxes to hinder black voting. Many states also require literacy tests, but all have loopholes to allow poor or illiterate whites to vote.

- In Massachusetts, where blacks had made their greatest political gains in the previous two decades, all black representatives have been voted out of the state legislature. Northern states have enacted many protective laws for blacks, but few are enforced.

- Cook and Dunbar collaborate with well-known performers Bert Williams and George Walker to produce the musical comedy *In Dahomey*. After spectacular success on Broadway, on the road, and in London, the show is performed at Buckingham Palace for England's king Edward VII.

1903
- Trotter confronts Washington during a speech, publicizing black opposition to accommodation; Washington has Trotter jailed for a month.

- Dismayed by the continuing oppression of black people, Du Bois shifts from the accommodationist to the Radical camp. *The Souls of Black Folk*, his eloquent criticism of Washington's conciliatory behavior, reverberates through the black community.

1905
- Du Bois convenes a meeting of Radicals at Niagara Falls; the Niagara Movement is formed to combat Washington's excessive influence and agitate against segregation, disfranchisement, and racial violence, thus becoming the first African American organization committed exclusively to fighting racial oppression. Washington reacts with a series of sabotage attempts, such as bribing newspapers to ignore the burgeoning movement.

- In Chicago, Robert Abbott founds a black newspaper, the *Defender*, which soon becomes known as the most militant black publication.

- Madam C. J. Walker develops a line of black hair-care products and markets them door-to-door. Within a few years, she will be the nation's first black female millionaire.

1906
- In Brownsville, Texas, black soldiers respond to repeated racial taunts with physical violence; three whites die in the ensuing shootout. President Roosevelt orders dishonorable discharges for three full companies of black soldiers; the decision will not be reversed until 1972.

- In Atlanta, one of the worst race riots in the country's history erupts as white men rip into blacks to avenge fictional attacks on white women. The Atlanta police provide no protection to blacks and even assist the attackers.

- The Odd Fellows, the largest black fraternal order, boasts 4,000 lodges and investments worth $3 million. Fraternal orders and mutual aid societies sometimes turn into businesses, such as John Merrick's North Carolina Mutual Life Insurance Company.

1907
- At the Boston meeting of the Niagara Movement, Du Bois and Trotter have a serious disagreement, and Trotter leaves the organization. Reacting to racial violence only with words, the movement's strength wanes; it dissolves in 1910.

1908
- In Springfield, Illinois, a white woman's false rape charges against a black man ignite a race riot. White mobs assault every black in their path; northern white liberals are disturbed by the vehement racism in their own region.

- William Howard Taft is elected president and allows segregation in some federal buildings for the first time.

- To the dismay of white racists, Jack Johnson becomes the first black heavyweight champion of the world.

1909
- Mary White Ovington, a white social worker and journalist, joins with other liberal whites in arranging a conference on racial discrimination; all the leading figures from the Niagara Movement except Trotter attend the interracial meeting. The New York conference gives birth to the National Association for the Advancement of Colored People (NAACP), the nation's first major civil rights organization. Du Bois becomes editor of the group's newspaper, the *Crisis*, but the rest of the organization's initial leadership is white. With strong grass-roots support, skilled legal action, and adept publicity, the NAACP plays a key role in gaining civil rights.

1

SEPARATE AND UNEQUAL

IT was July 1890, and Louis Martinet and Rudolphe Desdunes were disgusted. Their state, Louisiana, had just passed a law requiring blacks and whites to be segregated on trains. They knew that this law did not reflect the mutual desires of the two races; instead, it reflected the desire of white people to keep blacks separate and thereby to stigmatize and humiliate them. And that was not all. Although the law called for the separate accommodations to be equal, in fact most train companies supplied inferior service for blacks, failing to make any first-class cars available to them at any price.

Martinet, a black lawyer and newspaper man, and Desdunes, a black poet and historian, had already been excluded from white hotels, restaurants, theaters, schools, and libraries in their native city of New Orleans. Even though most American blacks were then afraid to challenge segregation—because of frequent violence against those who protested white dominance—Martinet and Desdunes decided they could no longer sit idly by. "The next thing . . . is to test the constitutionality of this law," Martinet declared. "We'll make a case, a test case, and bring it

Entitled The First Vote, *this engraving shows recently liberated slaves (one of them in the uniform of the victorious Union army) preparing to cast their ballots after the Civil War. During Reconstruction (1865–77), blacks captured 16 seats in the U.S. Congress and almost 200 in state legislatures.*

17

before the federal courts on the ground of the invasion of the right of a person to travel through the states unmolested."

The men's first step was to gather funds. Then, with 16 like-minded black Louisianans, they formed a group: the Citizens' Committee to Test the Constitutionality of the Separate Car Law. Finally, on October 10, 1891, they hired a lawyer to represent them. Because few southern lawyers felt sympathetic to black interests, the committee had to range far afield to get their man. He turned out to be Albion W. Tourgée, a somewhat eccentric white attorney from Ohio.

During Reconstruction, the period after the Civil War (1865–1877), Tourgée had been branded a carpetbagger—a term for northerners who moved to the postwar South to take advantage of the power vacuum left by the Confederacy's defeat. But unlike many who headed south to make money, Tourgée went for altruistic reasons: as a radical Republican, he sought to make life better for freed slaves. He had moved from Ohio to North Carolina, where he served as a judge and helped rewrite the state constitution. But he really made a name for himself by writing a series of novels about the Reconstruction experience. By the time Martinet and Desdunes contacted him, Tourgée was one of few northern whites still interested in black causes. He wrote a weekly newspaper column attacking segregation and had formed a small biracial civil rights group called the National Citizens Rights Association.

Joining Martinet and Desdunes in New Orleans, Tourgée conceived a plan to test the train-segregation law. He persuaded a light-skinned black man named Homer Adolph Plessy to violate the law so that Tourgée could contest it in the courts. And so on June 7, 1892, Homer Plessy purchased a first-class railroad ticket from New Orleans to Covington, Louisiana. Once on board, he sat down in a car reserved

for whites. Because maintaining separate cars for blacks and whites was expensive, the railroad company was more than willing to help set up a test case. Thus, railroad detective Christopher Cain promptly arrested Plessy and filed charges in New Orleans criminal court.

Appearing before Judge John H. Ferguson, Tourgée argued that Plessy should not be convicted because the segregation law he had broken violated the U.S. Constitution. But Ferguson rejected this reasoning, and Plessy was declared guilty. Tourgée immediately appealed to the state supreme court of Louisiana. It was at this point that the case got its name of *Plessy v. Ferguson*, because the state high court was to decide between the assertions of the defendant and the judge.

The Louisiana chief justice, Francis Nicholls, had himself signed the segregation law as governor in 1890, and he naturally sided with Ferguson, upholding

Black travelers gather around the "Colored Waiting Room" in the Jacksonville, Florida, railroad station at the turn of the century. By 1892, when black Louisianan Homer Plessy was forcibly removed from the whites-only section of a train, most southern states had enacted laws requiring racial separation in all public places.

Plessy's conviction. In explaining his decision, Nicholls pointed to several rulings by lower courts in which separate facilities for whites and blacks had been deemed acceptable as long as they were equal. "We have been at pains to expound this statute," the court wrote, "because the dissatisfaction felt with it by a portion of the people seems to us so unreasonable that we can account for it only on the ground of some misconception."

Next, Tourgée entreated the justices of the U.S. Supreme Court to hear the case. They agreed, but only after a three-year delay. Tourgée was happy about the delay because he felt it would give his side time to rally public opinion behind their mission.

In challenging the Louisiana law, Tourgée and Plessy were in fact challenging an extensive system of segregation that pervaded the South during the 1890s. This network of segregation laws had emerged gradually and irregularly. Initially segregation was a matter of custom, only later gaining legal reinforcement. Not until the 1890s did segregation in law, as opposed to segregation in practice, become the norm. What is more, segregation materialized at different times in different aspects of life. It first cropped up in education—by 1878 the majority of southern states required segregation in schools—and then in transportation. The first railroad-segregation law was instituted by Tennessee in 1881. By 1891, all but three southern states had passed laws similar to the one Homer Plessy was disputing.

Some southern states moved relatively slowly in separating the races. At the same time Plessy was denied his first-class seat in Louisiana, blacks in other southern states could still get served in white restaurants and bury their dead in white cemeteries. Segregation laws were intended not only to humiliate blacks but also to cut them off from employment opportunities and essential social services. In most cases, blacks received inferior facilities. In education, for example, when schools were segregated, white schools were invariably better staffed and funded.

The rise of segregation partly reflected a struggle for power among rival political factions. In an attempt to attract white votes, Republicans, Democrats, and Populists competed to see who could appear most racist. Some white politicians supported segregation more out of practical politics than racial hatred. Segregation was also motivated by economic factors. The poor whites who comprised the Populist party's ranks feared losing their jobs to blacks; thus they favored segregation in education and employment as a way of staving off economic competition. But the expansion of southern segregation was predominantly driven by racial prejudice. The majority of southern whites believed that blacks were innately inferior and should therefore have fewer rights, less political authority, and less wealth than whites.

Segregation laws were only one of several means by which whites held blacks down at the end of the 19th century. Whites also maneuvered to deprive blacks of their constitutional right to vote. Initially this was done by informal means—threats of violence, acts of violence, fraud, and economic pressure. But by the time the Supreme Court heard the Plessy case, state governments had begun using legal measures to keep blacks from voting. In 1890, Mississippi enacted a constitutional amendment that effectively disfranchised most of the state's blacks; the amendment required voters to pay a poll tax of two dollars and pass a literacy test. In 1895, South Carolina went one step

A newspaper cartoon from the late 1870s shows members of a southern racist organization, the White League, preventing blacks from casting their ballots. Protected by federal troops, former slaves voted freely during Reconstruction, but as soon as the army left, whites moved to suppress black rights.

further. To curtail the black vote, the state imposed a property requirement in addition to a poll tax and literacy test.

Another weapon with which southern whites maintained their grip on power was lynching, the murder of blacks by white vigilante mobs. Ostensibly the aim of lynchings was to punish blacks for violent crimes such as rape or murder, but in fact the aim was usually to terrorize them into silent submission to white dominance. Lynchings reached a peak during the 1880s and 1890s, when they occurred at a rate of 100 a year.

Because blacks were for the most part shut out of the judicial system, they had little recourse against lynching. In most southern states blacks were denied their constitutional right to serve on juries. Partly as a consequence of this, the black prison population shot up dramatically during the late 19th century; between 1865 and 1900 the number of imprisoned blacks in the Deep South increased sevenfold. Many of the black

Evidence of their grisly night's work behind them, members of an 1884 lynch mob ride away from their latest "defense of white womanhood." Most racial murders were based on false claims of black-on-white sexual assault.

A sharecropping couple in Savannah, Georgia, farms with the implements available to them, a primitive wooden plow and their own bones and muscle. In the 1890s, most employed southern blacks were either tenant farmers or sharecroppers; all were desperately poor.

inmates were jailed on trumped-up charges, so that southern governments could generate revenue by leasing them out to private employers. During the 1880s Alabama and Tennessee each added $100,000 to its treasury through the leasing of inmates to mining companies alone.

With so many forces arrayed against them, blacks had a difficult time improving their economic status. In 1890, 9 out of every 10 black workers held low-paying jobs in agriculture and domestic work. The bulk of southern black men were tenant farmers or sharecroppers. Although they paid a huge percentage of their crops in rent and were almost always in debt, the tenant farmers were slightly better off than the sharecroppers because they rented their own land and owned their own crops. Sharecroppers' lives were even worse because they were defined as mere laborers, earning a percentage of the crop they harvested as wages. But both groups were impoverished and virtually imprisoned by the debt they had to incur to buy food and supplies.

All these various forms of oppression combined to form a comprehensive system of racial subordination. This system has become known to history as Jim Crow—the name of a character from minstrel, or "blackface," shows. In taking the Louisiana law to the Supreme Court, Plessy and Tourgée were challenging not just segregation but the whole Jim Crow system.

The dire circumstances that blacks faced during the 1890s represented a sharp decline from their prospects during Reconstruction. In that period the Republicans—who had led the North to victory in the Civil War—dominated the federal government, and they used their power to guarantee the rights of the South's newly liberated blacks. During the first postwar years, the Republican Congress forced the South to accept the Constitution's 14th Amendment, which granted citizenship and full civil rights to blacks, and the 15th Amendment, which gave black men the vote. (No American woman would gain the vote until 1920.)

In 1871, Congress passed legislation establishing federal protection for black voting rights, and in the Civil Rights Act of 1875 it prohibited segregation in transportation, hotels, theaters, and in "other places of amusement." To provide education, food, health care, and legal assistance to former slaves, legislators created the Freedmen's Bureau. To ensure that Reconstruction initiatives were implemented, they dispatched federal troops to occupy the South. They also took the vote away from supporters of the Confederacy, a move that enabled a coalition of northerners, blacks, and southern Republicans to take control of southern state governments.

Under the new regime, blacks attained a fair amount of political power. Between 1869 and 1880 they captured 16 congressional seats and almost 200 in state legislatures, and in South Carolina they actually gained a majority. But by the mid-1870s northern Republicans were no longer focused on the protection of southern blacks. Their change of heart stemmed from several causes: the party had become more conservative, and its leaders had been distracted by problems caused by the economic panic of 1873. Many Republicans, furthermore, had come to believe that federal authority had gone much too far during Reconstruction.

When the 1877 presidential election ended in a tie, then, the opposing political parties made a deal. The Democrats agreed to accept the Republican candidate, Rutherford B. Hayes, as president; in return, the Republicans agreed to end federal intervention in southern affairs. The sudden absence of federal restraint left southern racists free to repress blacks to their hearts' desire.

When Plessy and Tourgée took their case to the Supreme Court, they hoped to halt this retreat from the gains of Reconstruction. Unfortunately, however, the Court's recent actions suggested only a dim hope for success. The amendments passed during Reconstruction had been specifically aimed at preventing discrimination against blacks, but the high court had systematically refused to apply them, in several cases ruling in favor of white supremacists. In an 1876 case that involved several lynchings in Louisiana, *United States v. Cruikshank,* the Court concluded that the 14th Amendment did not protect the civil rights of blacks from being violated by individuals. The amendment only applied to actions by state governments, the court ruled. Chief Justice Morrison Waite wrote that the amendment "adds nothing to the rights of one citizen as against another."

In the *Civil Rights Cases* of 1883, which concerned segregated seating at the New York City Opera, the Court extended this principle. Not only did the 14th Amendment not apply to individuals, the justices declared, it did not apply to the federal government either. Thus the federal government had no obligation to protect the rights of blacks, and therefore the 1875 Civil Rights Act, the Court said, was unconstitutional. There was, however, one reason for Tourgée and Plessy to be hopeful: they were challenging a state law, and the 14th Amendment did seem to apply.

Tourgée submitted his brief to the Supreme Court in October 1895. He asked the court to nullify the Louisiana statute on several grounds. First, he argued, the law deprived his client, Plessy, of property without due process of law—that property being "the reputation of being white." Such a reputation was necessary to attain wealth, prestige, and opportunity in the South, Tourgée said. In addition, Tourgée contested the statute as incompatible with the 13th Amendment, which not only abolished slavery but prohibited the re-creation of the conditions of servitude. The latter, Tourgée asserted, was exactly what segregation had done: it had established a new form of bondage.

Finally, Tourgée charged that the Louisiana law conflicted with the 14th Amendment, in that segregation reduced blacks to a subordinate position, while the amendment called for all citizens to be equal under the law. He rejected the contention by supporters of the law that it was impartial. "The object of such a law," he asserted, "is simply to debase and distinguish" the black race. He reminded the court that separate facilities established for blacks were almost never equal to those set up for whites. And he wondered

Their businesslike manner underscoring the horror of their actions, vigilantes— self-appointed lawmen— prepare to take the life of Jesse Washington, a mentally retarded 18-year-old accused of killing a white woman in Texas. In the 19th century's last decades, lynch mobs killed at least 100 African Americans each year.

whether there would ever be any end to segregation laws, if the Louisiana law was deemed constitutional:

> Why not require every white man's house to be painted white and every colored man's black? Why may it not require every white man's vehicle to be of one color and compel the colored citizen to use one of different color on the highway? Why not require every white business man to use a white sign and every colored man who solicits customers a black one?

Tourgée finished his appeal by saying, "Justice is pictured blind and her daughter, the Law, ought at least to be color-blind." The Supreme Court handed down its decision on May 18, 1896. Despite Tourgée's eloquence, the court, by a 7–1 vote, rejected Tourgée's arguments and upheld the Louisiana law. Segregation, said the justices, was acceptable as long as conditions were equal for blacks and whites. Thus the ruling became known as the "Separate but Equal" decision. The majority opinion was written by Justice Henry Billings Brown of Michigan. Brown maintained that segregation did not "necessarily imply the inferiority of either race." If segregation stamped blacks with "a badge of inferiority," he wrote, "it is solely because the colored race chooses to put that construction on it." Finally, he averred that the 14th Amendment had "not been intended to enforce a co-mingling of the races."

The lone dissenter, a former slave owner from Kentucky named John Marshall Harlan, wrote a minority opinion that offered a passionate but cogent rebuttal of Brown's decision. Harlan held all segregation laws to be clear attempts to degrade blacks and hold them down. The laws, he wrote, reflected the fact that "the white race deems itself to be the dominant race." He called the argument that segregation did not necessarily connote inferiority a "thin disguise" that would "not mislead anyone." And whereas those laws sought to bolster the dominance of whites, he contended, in the view of the Constitution, "there is in this country no superior, dominant ruling class of citizens. There is no caste here. Our Constitution . . . neither knows nor tolerates classes among citizens."

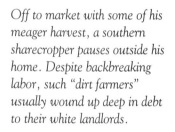

Off to market with some of his meager harvest, a southern sharecropper pauses outside his home. Despite backbreaking labor, such "dirt farmers" usually wound up deep in debt to their white landlords.

Thus, in Harlan's view, the Louisiana transportation law, and all others like it, were unconstitutional. Harlan saw the *Plessy* decision as being as "pernicious as the Dred Scott case," an 1857 ruling in which the Supreme Court had declared that blacks were not citizens of the United States.

In two ways, Harlan's dissent seemed to predict the future. First, it anticipated many of the arguments that the Supreme Court would make in finally overturning Plessy in 1954. Second, Harlan accurately foresaw that the decision would encourage racial prejudice, that it would foster the spread of Jim Crow. Indeed, in the wake of *Plessy*, many southern governments that had been uncertain about the constitutionality of

segregation laws hastened to pass them. In addition, the decision prompted the passage of a flurry of dis-franchisement laws—of which there had been only a few in 1896. If the justices were not opposed to segre-gation, southern whites reasoned, why would they object if blacks were deprived of the vote?

Ultimately, the *Plessy* decision served as a solid underpinning for Jim Crow, fortifying it with federal sanction. It marked a climactic step in the federal government's retreat from the Reconstruction-era policy of protecting blacks. For African Americans, it was an ominous development. If they could no longer count on the federal government to help them, to whom could they turn?

2

THE AGE OF
ACCOMMODATION

I N the first years after the *Plessy* decision, few
blacks resisted or even protested Jim Crow, the
array of humiliations and injustices designed to keep
blacks in "their place." Following the counsel of its
leaders—Booker T. Washington and other conserva-
tives—the black community adopted a strategy of
accommodation, not challenge, as the way to get
along with the white world. Strengthening the appeal
of the appeasement route were stories about the fate
of blacks who had demanded their rights: violent
death at the hands of a lynch mob. The accommodationist approach, then, owed its ascendancy both to
fear of reprisal and to the extraordinary influence of
Booker T. Washington.

Washington believed that blacks should bypass
political agitation and concentrate on economic self-
help. Rather than fight segregation, Washington
asserted, blacks should accept it and use isolation from
whites to improve themselves, establishing their own

Booker T. Washington makes a typically expressive gesture
during a speech at Tuskegee Institute, the vocational college he
founded in 1881. A schoolteacher in 1875, Washington had
become the most powerful black man in America by 1895.

33

Tuskegee staff members check out the Agricultural School on Wheels, one means of extending the college's research programs to poor black farmers. Committed to practical, hands-on training, Booker T. Washington declared that education should "fit us for the work around us."

schools, businesses, and other institutions. Once blacks had reached a certain level of achievement, Washington argued, whites would be forced to grant them respect and accept them as equal partners in an integrated society.

Washington's background as an educator and
self-made man helped shape his economic views.
Born a Virginia slave in 1856, he had been freed

by the Emancipation Proclamation in 1863. His family's extreme poverty forced him to go to work young; at nine, he took a job in a salt furnace, and later in his childhood toiled in a coal mine. Realizing that if he wanted to escape a life of grinding poverty, he would have to get an education, he taught himself to read with Webster's "blue-back" spelling book. The boy, who never knew his father's identity and who started life simply as "Booker," adopted the name of the nation's first president to serve as inspiration on his quest for self-improvement. At the age of 16, he walked almost 500 miles across Virginia to enroll at the Hampton Institute. Hampton offered blacks "industrial education," meaning that it stressed practical, moneymaking skills such as farming and brick making, rather than literature, math, and science. But the school's founder, Samuel Chapman Armstrong, also directed the instructors to teach manners, morals, and such values as thrift, honesty, faithfulness, accuracy, and persistence. Washington came away from his years at Hampton a disciple of this kind of education.

After graduating, Washington became a teacher himself, first in Malden, West Virginia, then back at Hampton. He so distinguished himself that in 1881 he was hired as the first president of a new industrial school for blacks in Tuskegee, Alabama. At first he had few resources to work with: two small buildings and a tiny staff of teachers. But when he left 34 years later, Tuskegee Institute, as it had come to be called, boasted 100 buildings and 200 teachers.

Washington had proved an excellent administrator and superb fund-raiser. He also managed to overcome the initial hostility of local whites, assuring them that the school had no intention of disrupting the community, but aimed instead to help develop the local economy. When whites saw that Tuskegee's industrial program indeed produced a useful pool of menial labor, and that its students supplied the city with much produce and many services, their resistance dissolved.

Eventually, Washington concluded that the approach that had worked so well in Tuskegee—vocational education and mollification of whites—could benefit black people as a whole. To gather support for this approach, he established connections with other black educators, newspaper publishers, and community leaders. He also began making speeches to explain his philosophy. He repeatedly championed practical education; for example, he declared that "for years to come the education of the people of my race should be so directed that the greatest proportion of the mental strength of the masses will be brought to bear upon the everyday practical things of life." But like his mentor, Armstrong, he held that just as important as practical skills were traits like moral uprightness, thrift, cleanliness, and willingness to work hard.

Washington's influence steadily grew. In 1895, he became the first black person to address a major convention of southern white leaders, delivering a speech at the Cotton States and International Exposition in Atlanta. The speech not only established him as the country's preeminent black leader, it furnished a clear outline of his principles. He took pains to absolve white people of responsibility for the degradation of southern blacks; racism, he asserted, was minimal. The racism that did exist, he insisted, was the fault of blacks themselves, an inevitable consequence of their backwardness. The solution to blacks' problems was clear; they needed to escape poverty and ignorance through education and economic accumulation.

Washington, a genius at fund raising, brings millionaires and cultural leaders together at a 1906 Tuskegee conference. At right is Harvard University president Charles Eliot; standing between him and Washington is immensely wealthy industrialist Andrew Carnegie.

Washington maintained that eventually economic and moral improvement among blacks would impel whites to grant them equal political rights and would lead to desegregation. It was a gradualist solution: equality would not be achieved overnight. In the meantime, Washington renounced any intention of contesting segregation. "In all things that are purely social," he said, "we can be as separate as the fingers, yet one as the hand in all matters essential to progress." He similarly condoned obstacles to black voting, maintaining that literacy and property requirements would encourage blacks to seek schooling and material prosperity.

Washington's speech, later dubbed the "Atlanta Compromise" by critics, elevated his standing primarily because his message had strong appeal for southern whites. From then on, they acknowledged him as the main spokesman for blacks, which in turn increased his prominence in the eyes of blacks. Southern whites liked what they heard from Washington because of his apparent lack of interest in disturbing the status quo. What they did not realize was that he endorsed Jim Crow only in the short run, to remove distractions from the effort to improve blacks' economic position. They mistook his means for his end.

After the *Plessy* decision, Washington extended his reach further. He worked to increase his support among the northern white elite. And indeed many northern businessmen and politicians were drawn to his accommodationist approach because they thought it would ease racial conflict in the South, thereby making the area a more fertile ground for economic development. Washington's success in endearing himself to this group was manifested, for example, by his receipt in June 1896 of an honorary master's degree from Harvard University, a bastion of the northeastern old guard. He was the first black to receive such an honor from Harvard.

Washington's primary motivation for seeking greater leverage with the northeastern elite was to raise money for black education. From the time Tuskegee was founded, he had displayed a gift for getting

*The Wizard of Tuskegee—
George Washington Carver
(second from right)—teaches a
botany class around 1898. An
ecologist before the word became
fashionable, Carver taught
that everything in nature is
interrelated; his fame rested on
his discovery of hundreds of
new uses for the peanut,
the sweet potato, and other
common southern crops.*

donations for his and other black schools from northern philanthropists. For example, he had secured several gifts from the Slater Fund, a trust established by textile magnate John Slater. But in the late 1890s Washington stepped up his efforts. In 1899, he launched a major fund-raising drive for Tuskegee with a benefit at New York City's Madison Square Garden. The event brought out many of the city's leading lights, including politician and reformer Carl Schurz and financiers J. P. Morgan and John D. Rockefeller— who each immediately pledged $10,000. Soon thereafter, Washington persuaded millionaire industrialist and philanthropist Andrew Carnegie to give $600,000 in U.S. Steel bonds for black schooling.

At the same time, Washington began to exert greater leverage in national politics. In 1897, President William McKinley seriously considered making Washington a member of his cabinet until Washington stated that he was not interested: "McKinley has no position within his gift that I would think of accepting were it offered," he said. Washington scored a major public-relations coup when he persuaded McKinley to visit Tuskegee in December 1898.

Washington's stature was also enhanced by the achievements of George Washington Carver, whom he hired in 1896 to head an agricultural training program at Tuskegee. Carver quickly built a reputation as the most distinguished agricultural scientist in the country.

At an August 1900 conference in Boston, Washington set up the National Negro Business League, an important step in his campaign to promote black business. The gathering was attended by about 400 representatives from 34 states, who elected Washington as the league's first president.

Washington's activities in philanthropy, politics, education, and the stimulating of business enlarged his power to such a degree that by 1900 he had built a network of alliances that was the equivalent of a political machine; his power base was, in fact, sometimes referred to as the "Tuskegee Machine." Like a political boss, he employed calculating and sometimes ruthless methods. For example, he used his control of philanthropic funds for education to force heads of black schools to toe the accommodationist line. Similarly, he used meetings of the Negro Business League to recruit lieutenants for his machine so that he would have loyal forces in all black population centers. He controlled the black press by presenting generous donations—some people called them "hush money"—to newspapers that agreed not to oppose his policies. He even went so far as to hire secret agents to infiltrate and spy on rival organizations.

Washington has been sharply criticized for the fact that his accommodationist approach encouraged white oppression of blacks and prolonged the career of Jim Crow. But to be fair to Washington, it should also be noted that although he always publicly disavowed protest, he supported it privately. For example, he secretly funneled thousands of dollars into court cases disputing voting restrictions against blacks. And he quietly hired a lobbyist who helped block a bill that would have led to railroad segregation in the North. Moreover, although Washington ostensibly disapproved of black political activity, he himself constantly cultivated relationships with powerful politicians.

The majority of black leaders followed Booker T. Washington's example and voiced little opposition to Jim Crow during the last years of the 19th century. But a handful of intrepid men and women adopted a more confrontational approach. Black journalist Ida B. Wells, for example, was probably the most outspoken foe of racial discrimination during the late 1890s. Wells concentrated in particular on combating the pernicious crime of lynching.

The courage and independence that enabled Wells to pursue a lonely strategy of protest exhibited themselves early on, during her youth in Mississippi. After her parents, both former slaves, died of yellow fever in 1878, Wells, who was only 16 at the time and the eldest of eight children, chose to raise her siblings by herself, taking a job as a teacher in order to support the family.

Journalist Ida Wells-Barnett (left) comforts the widow and children of a lynch victim—a young Memphis grocer whose success led jealous white competitors to kill him and his two partners in 1892. The tragedy sparked Wells-Barnett's lifelong crusade against racial injustice.

Wells tested discriminatory practices for the first time in 1884 in Memphis, where she had moved to find a better job. On a train ride to her teaching job, a conductor asked her to leave the first-class car, even though she had a first-class ticket, because of regulations requiring whites and blacks to travel in separate cars. When she refused to move, the conductor and two white passengers picked her up and carried her off the train. She successfully sued the railroad company, receiving $500 in damages, but a higher court overturned the verdict in 1887. Nevertheless, some good did come of the experience: articles she wrote about the lawsuit for a church newspaper helped earn her a position as editor of the *Memphis Free Speech and Headlight*, a small Baptist weekly newspaper of which she later became a part owner.

But it was not until 1892, in response to an ugly incident in Memphis, that Wells pledged herself full-time to the struggle for black equality. The incident began when three young black men, all close friends of Wells, were kidnapped by whites and carried on a railway engine to the outskirts of the city. The three blacks were then shot dead, solely because their grocery business had presented competition to a nearby white grocery store.

Outraged by this lynching, Wells wrote editorials in the *Free Speech* in which she urged blacks to pack up their belongings and flee Memphis. The city, she asserted, would "neither protect our lives and property, nor give us a fair trial in the courts." Black residents heeded her call en masse. White civic leaders, concerned that the black exodus might injure local businesses, demanded that Wells recant her advice, but this only stiffened her resolve. She answered with an editorial denouncing lynching. Deciding that Wells had gone too far, proponents of white supremacy formed a mob and ransacked the offices of her newspaper.

Fortunately, at the time of the attack Wells was in New York, visiting T. Thomas Fortune, editor of the black newspaper *New York Age*. Realizing that it would be too dangerous for her to return to Memphis, she accepted Fortune's offer to write for his publication. She used this position as a springboard from which to launch a major crusade against lynching. In addition to a steady stream of antilynching articles, she delivered speeches throughout the Northeast and began writing books, publishing in 1895 *A Red Record: Tabulated Statistics and Alleged Causes of Lynchings in the United States, 1892–1894*. In the process she provided the nation with a detailed record of white-on-black murder, producing names, dates, places, and motives for thousands of killings.

> Wells made clear that the charges made by white assailants to justify their crimes were almost always spurious. While lynchers frequently claimed they had simply been punishing blacks for committing rape or murder, in fact, Wells revealed, the motive was usually just to terrorize blacks, to scare them into accepting their inferior status. Wells's writings on lynchings and rape were especially daring. Approximately one-third of all lynchings resulted from claims that black men had raped white women. But in most such cases, Wells insisted, the white woman had willingly developed a relationship with a black man, making a rape accusation only because of fear or pressure by other whites.

In 1895, Wells married Ferdinand Barnett and moved to Chicago, and the next year she had her first child. But in spite of her new roles as wife and mother, she kept up her relentless battle against racial murders in the years after the *Plessy* decision. On occasion, she had to bring nursing babies along on her lecturing tours. Of her multiple roles she said, "I found that motherhood was a profession by itself, just like school teaching and lecturing, and that once one was launched on such a career she owed it to herself to become as expert as possible in the practice of her profession." To spread her antilynching message further, Wells-Barnett and her husband established a newspaper in Chicago called the *Conservator*.

In 1898, after a particularly horrible lynching in which the black postmaster of Anderson, South Carolina, was killed, outraged Chicago blacks gave Wells-

Barnett funds to travel to Washington to lobby for antilynching legislation. She spent five weeks in the capital, meeting daily with members of a committee that was considering a bill that proposed to compensate the postmaster's survivors. The high point of the trip came when Wells-Barnett persuaded President McKinley to meet with her. He expressed sympathy for her cause and assured her that he had dispatched some of his best secret-service agents to hunt for the postmaster's killers. But by the end of the year, because of the outbreak of the Spanish-American War and the unwillingness of northern congressmen to alienate their southern colleagues, the compensatory bill had been withdrawn, and the wider antilynching legislation advocated by Wells-Barnett had never even been taken up.

Such setbacks did not stop Wells-Barnett from continuing her mission. In 1900, she conducted an in-depth investigation into a lynching in Missouri. And the same year, she published *Mob Rule in New Orleans*, a history of racial violence in that city.

Although lynching was Wells-Barnett's primary focus, she also spoke out against other aspects of Jim Crow, and she contributed to the development of important black institutions. In 1898, she helped revive the Afro-American League, a national organization dedicated to bringing greater black unity. The idea of reactivating the league, which had been founded in 1890 but had been defunct for several years, came from Wells-Barnett's old friend T. Thomas Fortune. To her dismay, she soon discovered that he wanted it to assume Washington's posture of compromise. At the inaugural meeting in Rochester, New York, according to Wells-Barnett's autobiography, Fortune "spent more time trying to point out the shortcomings of the race than in encouraging unification." Wells-Barnett and her allies, however, managed to steer the league on the more radical course of agitating against Jim Crow. Wells-Barnett herself

Wealthy feminist Mary Church Terrell, elected first president of the National Association of Colored Women (NACW) in 1896, was perhaps best described as a conservative reformer; although far more radical than Booker T. Washington, she was considerably less militant than Ida Wells-Barnett.

was elected secretary of the organization, whose members renamed it the Afro-American Council.

In November 1898, the council held an emergency meeting following a race riot in Wilmington, North Carolina. It issued a resolution criticizing President McKinley for not condemning Wilmington whites for inciting the riot. Wells-Barnett declared at the meeting, "If this gathering means anything, it means that we have at last come to a point in our race history where we must do something for ourselves and do it now. We must educate the white people out of their 250 years of slave history." In taking a militant stand against oppression, the Afro-American Council was one of the first black protest groups to work on a national scale. But its following remained small, and

Sporting his trademark black bow tie, Booker T. Washington stands front and center at the first annual meeting of the National Negro Business League (NNBL), held in Boston, Massachusetts, in 1900. Washington founded the organization to promote the interests of black businessmen, and to teach enterprising blacks how to climb the nation's economic ladder.

its strong words were not accompanied by strong actions such as lawsuits or boycotts.

Wells-Barnett was also instrumental in the creation of a national network of black women's clubs. Earlier in the 1890s she had given lectures in New York City and Boston, inspiring the women of those cities to form their own clubs. In 1895, Wells-Barnett herself set up a Chicago women's club, whose members named it after her. Then in 1896, Wells-Barnett

helped to found the National Association of Colored Women (NACW), whose first president was Mary Church Terrell. Member of an elite family from Memphis, Tennessee, and heiress to a large fortune, Terrell used her post to fight discrimination. Strongly opposed to discrimination not only on the basis of race but also on the basis of gender, Terrell formed alliances with white feminist organizations. But Wells-Barnett was disappointed by Terrell's decision, in fighting racial discrimination, to pursue a middle course between Wells-Barnett's militancy and Washington's conservatism.

Wells-Barnett frequently criticized Booker T. Washington's accommodationist strategy during the late 1890s. She did agree with him on one point, however: that blacks should try to better themselves through economic self-help and thrift. She wrote in one article, "Let the [African American] continue to education, character, and above all, put money in his purse. When he has a dollar in his pocket and many more in the bank, he can move from injustice and oppression and no one can say to him nay." But unlike Washington, she did not think economic advancement by itself would make southern whites accept blacks as equals. The lynching of her three friends in Memphis had convinced her that merely attaining wealth would not bring equality. Economic action such as boycotts, she concluded, had to be employed as a lever to force hostile southern whites to change their behavior.

Surprisingly, Wells-Barnett remained on friendly terms with Washington for most of the 1890s, but their opposing views made conflict inevitable. In 1899, she decided she could no longer remain cordial after Washington made comments that seemed to condone several lynchings. At the annual gathering of the Afro-American Council in August of that year, she persuaded the members to issue a denunciation of Washington. Ultimately, however, the only person damaged by the attack was Wells-Barnett herself. It led her colleagues on the National Association of

Colored Women, most of whom supported Washington, to remove her from the group's leadership. For his part, Washington seemed little concerned. "Miss Wells," he sneered, "is fast making herself so ridiculous that everyone is getting tired of her."

At the turn of the century, then, in spite of Wells-Barnett's efforts, accommodation reigned supreme. Meanwhile, lynching had decreased only slightly. Nevertheless, Wells-Barnett had brought together an invaluable store of information that would eventually help turn the tide against lynching. And the tenacity and strength she demonstrated in her activities would serve as inspiration to the increasing number of black leaders who would question Washington's approach during the following decade.

In addition to challenges against Jim Crow by a handful of courageous black leaders such as Wells-Barnett, at the turn of the century a few scattered protests at the grassroots level took place around the country. Most of these protests were spontaneous local uprisings against segregation on streetcars. Between 1896 and 1906 blacks in about 30 southern cities conducted boycotts against transportation companies that had introduced separate seating areas for black riders. In four cities—Nashville, Chattanooga, Savannah, and Houston—blacks even formed new trolley services to offer alternatives to the segregated rail lines. Not widely noticed at the time and almost forgotten today, these protests marked an early application of the direct action tactics that the civil rights movement would use with great success during the 1950s and 1960s. But at the turn of the century the forces of reaction were too strong, and none of the boycotts achieved its goal.

3

JIM CROW SPREADS

HEEDING Booker T. Washington's conciliatory advice, blacks kept a low profile in the late 1890s. As a result, southern whites expanded Jim Crow. When the *Plessy* decision had been handed down, blacks in states of the Upper South could still sit on first-class train cars alongside whites. But in 1898, South Carolina enacted a law requiring blacks and whites to ride on separate cars. North Carolina followed suit in 1899, as did Virginia in 1900. During the same period, several states mandated segregation on streetcars for the first time.

Meanwhile, disfranchisement legislation, which had lagged behind segregation laws before *Plessy*, now caught up. Between 1896 and 1903 four more states— Louisiana, North Carolina, Alabama, and Virginia— amended their constitutions to require voters to pass literacy tests and pay poll taxes. This brought to six the number of states that effectively disfranchised blacks through such means. All the other southern states set up similar restrictions without amending their constitutions. By 1902, poll taxes had been introduced in every former Confederate state.

Men of the 9th Cavalry charge up Cuba's San Juan Hill during the Spanish American War. The all-black 9th and 10th cavalries impressed even hard-line racists: "I have never thought much of the colored man," said one southern officer after the 1898 war, "but now I feel differently toward them. I never saw such fighting as those 10th Cavalry men did."

Southern officials devised various loopholes to ensure that the new requirements did not keep poor whites from voting. In several states, ownership of property—which many poor whites had achieved but most blacks had not—exempted a man from the literacy requirement. In 1898, Louisiana instituted the South's first so-called grandfather clause; under an amendment to the state constitution, every male who had a forebear—in most cases a grandfather—who had been qualified to vote on January 1, 1867, was added to the list of registered voters. No blacks, of course, could make such a claim, but many poor whites who would otherwise have been denied the vote by poll taxes or literacy tests could. Alabama, North Carolina, and Maryland later adopted grandfather clauses as well.

Within a few years after the *Plessy* decision, the vast majority of blacks had been disfranchised. In Louisiana, for example, new requirements reduced the number of registered black voters from 130,000 in 1898 to 5,000 in 1902. In Alabama the number of blacks on the rolls shrank from 181,000 to 3,000 after new constitutional provisions took effect. Those few blacks who retained the franchise saw their votes become meaningless as "white primaries" became the norm.

Between 1896 and 1915 every southern state granted the Democratic party the right to exclude black voters from primaries, a move that leaders justified with the specious logic that political parties constituted private clubs and so were exempt from federal suffrage laws. Because of the Democratic party's dominance in the South during this period, its candidates almost always won general elections, and so its primaries usually represented the real contest.

Like segregation efforts, disfranchisement laws acquired the blessing of the Supreme Court. In 1898 the high court deemed poll taxes and literacy tests constitutional. And five years later, it went further and declared acceptable all suffrage restrictions not explicitly based on race, color, or previous subjection to slavery.

The spread of disfranchisement was also spurred by the rise of the Populist party in the South and by that party's power struggle with older white factions. Events that occurred in North Carolina typified this process. In 1896, the state's Populists established an alliance with black Republicans against the Democrats. Established for political gain rather than ideological conviction, the interracial alliance at first seemed mutually beneficial. Populists won many state offices, and a black Republican from North Carolina, George H. White, became the only member of his race elected to the U.S. Congress in 1896.

But in the 1898 elections the Democrats trounced the Populist-Republicans. Blaming their black allies for the defeat, white Populists soon attacked blacks in Wilmington, North Carolina, setting off the bitter race riot that the Afro-American Council later asked President McKinley to condemn. Once in power, the Democrats sought revenge against their black opponents by instituting a poll tax and a literacy test. White Populist leaders supported these moves. They also called for additional Jim Crow measures, deciding that they had to break their union with blacks and adopt an even more militantly racist stance than the Democrats in order to win the next election.

Conditions for blacks in the North were also getting worse during the late 1890s. This represented a

After burning the offices of the Record, *Wilmington, North Carolina's black newspaper, proud local whites line up for a souvenir photograph. The attack on the paper took place during a murderous 1898 racial rampage, triggered by reports that blacks had caused the defeat of white Populist party candidates; 20 African Americans died in the rioting.*

sharp turnabout from the 1880s, when there had been many hopeful signs for the 10 percent of the nation's blacks who lived above the Mason-Dixon line. During the 1880s the number of blacks holding office in northern state legislatures and city councils had risen dramatically, but during the following decade the number declined just as drastically. In Massachusetts, where blacks wielded their greatest political power, all black representatives had been voted out of the state legislature by 1902.

The 1880s had also seen northern state legislatures pass a flurry of protective laws for blacks. By 1883, all northern states had acknowledged the right of blacks to an education.

By 1890 most had prohibited segregation in public accommodations. But over the course of the
1890s enforcement of these laws became disturb-
ingly lax. Few cases were prosecuted, few fines
were levied, and in some places—such as lower
Ohio and other areas contiguous to the South—
officials refused to enforce the laws at all, allowing segregation to take over restaurants, hotels,
stores, and schools.

The intensification of discrimination by labor
unions during this decade also hurt northern blacks.
In fact, it hurt them more than it did blacks in the
South. Eighty percent of southern blacks lived in rural

Metalworkers ply their skills in a small St. Louis foundry around 1900. At this time, most labor unions accepted only whites, which made industrial jobs for skilled workers—with occasional exceptions such as these—almost nonexistent for blacks.

areas, where unions were irrelevant, but about 65 percent of northern blacks lived in cities, where they were dependent on unskilled jobs in heavy industry, an area over which labor unions exercised strong control. During the 1880s the Knights of Labor had been the dominant national labor organization; this group made a sincere effort to reach out to blacks, recruiting 60,000 black members by 1886.

But during the 1890s the Knights were eclipsed in importance by the American Federation of Labor, an alliance of trade unions that generally refused to admit black members, either as a matter of official policy or unspoken custom. These unions sometimes justified their exclusion of blacks by pointing to the frequent appearance of blacks as strikebreakers. In truth, however, blacks served as "scabs" only because discrimination prevented them from obtaining other kinds of

employment. Only in a few industries—notably rail-
roads and mining—was there much interracial coop-
eration among workers.

The spread of discriminatory practices in both the
North and the South around the turn of the century
was encouraged by the spread of ultraracist writings.
Not surprisingly, southern politicians—men such as
Governor Hoke Smith of Georgia and Governor J. K.
Vardaman of Mississippi—sought to justify their sup-
port of Jim Crow laws by publishing articles asserting
that blacks were innately inferior. Typical of these
articles' titles were *The Negro: A Beast* and *The Negro:
A Menace to Civilization*.

Surprisingly, these views were echoed by northern
academics in the biological and social sciences. A
number of anthropologists, for example, wrote dense
theoretical tracts supporting the astonishing proposi-
tion that the world's people could be divided into an
intricate racial hierarchy, with Anglo-Saxons at the
top and blacks at the bottom, barely above the apes.
This "scientific" racism even found its way into such
respectable magazines as *Harper's*, *Scribner's*, and the
Atlantic Monthly.

According to Rayford Logan, in his book *The
Negro in American Life and Thought*, blacks were
depicted in these publications as naturally "supersti-
tious, dull, stupid, imitative, ignorant, happy-go-
lucky, improvident, lazy, immoral, and criminal." The
growing influence of social Darwinism—the belief
that Darwin's "survival of the fittest" principle applied
to human society as well as to plant and animal
species—encouraged racist thinking in the late 19th
century. If, as social Darwinists held, biological superiority explained success in intergroup conflict, then,
many whites reasoned, whites must be biologically
superior because they held the dominant position in
society.

A large surge in immigration between 1880 and 1910 from countries such as Italy and Russia, which had previously sent few newcomers, also contributed to the rise of racism at the turn of the century. The new immigrants made many American whites of northern European ancestry fear that their culture might not continue to set the standard for the nation. The spread of racism was also pushed by a shift in American foreign policy during the 1890s. For more than 100 years the United States had engaged in few foreign engagements; now it adopted a new strategy of expansionism. To rationalize American intervention in, and annexation of, foreign lands such as Cuba and Hawaii, members of the Anglo-Saxon elite contended that whites, because of their innate superiority, were obliged to colonize darker peoples in order to uplift them. The phrase "white man's burden" became popular as a way of describing this supposed obligation.

Blacks were thus understandably ambivalent when their country entered the Spanish-American War in 1898. (Whipped up by the sensationalist American press, war fever swept the United States after a U.S. battleship mysteriously blew up in Havana, Cuba, then a Spanish colony. Declaring war against Spain, the United States quickly defeated Spanish forces, not only in Cuba but in the Spanish-held Philippine Islands. Lasting only a few months, the war ended with the United States in possession of Cuba, Puerto Rico, Guam, and the Philippines.)

Many blacks saw the Spanish-American War as the outgrowth of racist beliefs, and they lamented its results: the subjugation of black residents in several foreign lands. A large number of blacks, however, supported the war out of patriotism and loyalty to the Republican party (Republican president McKinley had led the country into the war). When

McKinley called for volunteers, thousands of blacks attempted to enlist. At first they were denied entry into the armed services because new units were being formed only from existing state militias. Blacks were banned from all southern state militias and made up only a minute portion of those in the North. Some blacks even organized their own regiments in an attempt to participate. Eventually, however, as a result of manpower shortages and lobbying by black leaders, Congress allowed the creation of 16 black regiments. But because most of the fighting ended within four months, black volunteers saw little action.

The only black troops heavily involved in combat belonged to four already existing black regiments. Formed after the Civil War to fight western Indian tribes, these units were based in the American West and were thus ill-prepared for the tropical terrain in which the Spanish-American War took place. Nevertheless, they served with great distinction on the Cuban front. Two black units, the 9th and 10th U.S. Cavalries, played a particularly important role, charging up San Juan Hill with Theodore Roosevelt's famed Rough Riders and helping them at the battle of Las Guasimas by opening holes in a Spanish fort.

Many participants credited the black cavalry units with saving the Rough Riders from being wiped out at Las Guasimas. "If it had not been for the Negro cavalry, the Rough Riders would have been exterminated," said one white southern officer. "I am not a Negro lover," he added, "but the Negroes saved that fight."

Captain Charles Young, seen here as a West Point cadet, was the only black officer in the U.S. Army when the Spanish-American War broke out. Black soldiers, however, fought with such distinction that many received field promotions; by the war's end, the number of black officers topped 100.

For his part, Roosevelt wavered in his response to his black comrades, a reaction that foreshadowed his mixed record on civil rights as president during the next decade. On one occasion Roosevelt said of the black troops, "The Spaniards called them 'smoked Yankees' but we found them to be an excellent breed of Yankees." But on another, he insinuated that they were cowards and that they had retreated, although the historical record showed they had not: "None of the white regulars of the Rough Riders showed the slightest sign of weakening; but under the strain, the colored infantrymen began to get a little uneasy and drift to the rear."

The courage of the black soldiers earned them more than praise. At one point in the war four men from the 10th Cavalry realized that 15 white soldiers had been cut off by the Spanish as they tried to land off the coast. The four commandeered a boat, rowed through an eruption of Spanish gunfire, loaded up the stranded troops, and pulled them to safety. All four were cited for gallantry, and each was awarded a Medal of Honor, the nation's highest decoration. Said one white eyewitness, "I am a southerner by birth, and I have never thought much of the colored man. But now I feel differently toward them. I never saw such fighting as those 10th Cavalry men did."

At the outset of the Spanish-American War the U.S. military boasted exactly one commissioned black officer, Captain Charles Young. By the end of the war more than 100 blacks had become officers. But in spite of their major contribution, black troops were kept segregated from whites throughout the war. Moreover, those who were stationed in the South before departing for the front were regularly harassed by local whites. A white newspaper editor in Georgia bragged that when black soldiers encamped there challenged the "color line" they were "promptly clubbed into submission." Nevertheless, the war was a beneficial experience for many blacks. It not only garnered them recognition for their heroism but helped them to understand fully their rights as Americans. For the first time, many came to realize that if men were willing to die for their country, that country should be willing to give them status as full citizens.

4

BUILDING INSTITUTIONS

BOOKER T. Washington's philosophy sometimes encouraged racial oppression, but it had a highly positive effect as well. Washington's emphasis on economic self-help and educational advancement spurred blacks to strengthen their own communities. The 20th century dawned on improved black schools, the expansion of black businesses, and a flowering of black culture. An impressive array of new institutions increased black pride and self-respect. These advances helped improve the quality of black lives in spite of setbacks in race relations.

The interaction of blacks with whites, however, comprises only one element of African American history. Even under the looming shadow of Jim Crow, many American blacks led fruitful and interesting lives, deriving satisfaction, for example, from strong bonds of community, a rich musical tradition, and a thriving black church. In fashioning their own community, blacks played an active role in shaping their own destiny during the late 1800s and early 1900s.

Tuskegee students stack bricks in 1902. Booker T. Washington's emphasis on vocational education—his students learned such skills as brickmaking, shoe repair, and carpentry— remained highly respected until about 1910, when expanding mechanization reduced the need for workers with such training.

In no area did turn-of-the-century African Americans invest more energy or respect than in education. Historian John Hope Franklin (in his celebrated book *From Slavery to Freedom: A History of Negro Americans*) observes that from the time of emancipation, black parents regarded school as "the greatest single opportunity to escape the indignities and proscriptions of an oppressive white south." Many parents made great sacrifices to obtain educations for their children: in spite of almost universal poverty, blacks spent more than $15 million on school tuition between 1870 and 1899.

In addition to these eager black parents, several other developments stimulated the growth of black education. One was an improvement in American education in general: 260 colleges were founded between 1860 and 1900. Another positive development, ironically, was the segregation of southern school systems. Compared with their white counterparts, black public schools had fewer class days, lower teacher salaries, and less money per student: in 1900, southern states annually spent about $9 for each white student and about $2 for each black student. The shortcomings of public schools prompted the creation of numerous private high schools and colleges for blacks.

In raising money for these institutions, black educators also benefited from the increasing interest of wealthy white northerners in black education. In 1903, oil magnate John D. Rockefeller set up the General Education Fund, an organization to which he eventually contributed $53 million to finance training programs for black public-school teachers. Between 1905 and 1907, Philadelphia heiress Anna T.

Jeanes placed part of her huge fortune—$1.2 million—in a foundation to support rural black schools. Meanwhile the Slater Fund, established in 1882, continued until 1911 to assist general programs at financially strapped public schools and teacher-training programs at black private schools.

Almost all blacks agreed that education was essential, but they disagreed about what kind was best. Some thought that liberal arts programs produced the most well-rounded individuals; others believed that vocational, or specific job-training, education was the best route. The latter group wanted to train black youngsters for service jobs—in farming, for example, or housekeeping—or for goods-production jobs—as shoemakers, printers, carpenters, and bricklayers—that would be in demand by the southern white population. Thanks to Booker T. Washington's strong influence and fund-raising abilities, vocational education ruled between 1890 and 1910. This pleased northern philanthropists, who assumed that such training would best prepare blacks for a productive role in expanding the southern economy. It also pleased southern whites, who were under the impression that the sole goal of vocational education was to train blacks for menial jobs that would keep them subordinate to whites. In fact, however, blacks who advanced vocational education saw it as a tool that would enable blacks to become upwardly mobile.

As it turned out, vocational programs had trouble attaining this latter goal. For one thing, study courses in this area were extremely expensive, and only a few schools—Tougaloo, Tuskegee, and Hampton—could afford to implement them properly. Moreover, the programs trained blacks for positions that were beginning to disappear: the increasing mechanization of industry was fast eliminating many skilled jobs, replacing them with assembly-line positions that required little or no skill.

College students attend a history class in 1902. At this point, schools for blacks and those for whites were far apart in quantity and quality, but the gulf was gradually shrinking; by 1900, 34 black schools were offering college programs.

At the same time, discriminatory practices by labor unions were also reducing the number of jobs for skilled black artisans. In the end, many graduates of industrial schools could find employment only as teachers of industrial education. Fortunately, several good colleges continued to offer liberal arts curricula; one of them, Spelman College, attracted enough financial aid from Rockefeller to make it number two in endowments among southern women's colleges.

By 1900, 1.5 million black children attended school and 28,500 blacks worked as teachers. College programs were offered by 34 black schools, including 4 black land-grant colleges in Virginia, Arkansas, Georgia, and Delaware, colleges that had been created by an 1890 act of Congress. Still, blacks had a long way to go before achieving parity with whites in education; for example, only 700 blacks were in college in 1900.

However limited, gains in education helped account for two other important changes in black society. As southern blacks began to acquire training in such fields as teaching, medicine, and law, along with cabinet making, and other kinds of artisanship, more and more moved to the urban areas where such abilities were most in demand. The growth of manufacturing in the South also lured blacks to the cities: between 1891 and 1910 the number of blacks working in southern industry rose from 7,000 to 350,000. By 1900, 28 percent of the black population lived in cities, up from 16 percent in 1860; six cities—Philadelphia, New York, Baltimore, Washington, Memphis, and New Orleans—had accumulated black populations larger than 50,000.

At the same time that blacks were becoming increasingly urbanized, opportunities in industry and the acquisition of professional skills were increasing. The combination sparked the emergence of a black middle class, a new bourgeoisie whose members—unlike the old black elite—were not all light-skinned or descended from house slaves or freedmen. It included teachers, doctors, ministers, civil servants, postal workers, railroad porters, and craftsmen.

The presence of sizable black communities in southern towns and cities fostered the development of black businesses. These companies were also spurred by Booker T. Washington's promotion of black entrepreneurship through the Negro Business League, as well as his policy of urging black customers

John Merrick (this page) and
Alonzo F. Herndon (right)
represented the cream of the
black business and professional
elite, a group beginning
to make its mark in America
at the turn of the century.
Both Merrick and Herndon
amassed their fortunes in the
insurance business.

to patronize black companies. New black businesses serving expanding black neighborhoods helped offset a sharp loss experienced in these communities: the demise of older black firms that had depended on a white clientele, and that had failed as growing racial prejudice soured whites on dealing with black businessmen.

The majority of new businesses were opened by small operators: barbers, storekeepers, artisans. But a few larger black concerns appeared in banking, insurance, and real estate. These companies benefited from white neglect of black customers. Between 1900 and 1911 the number of banks run by blacks increased from 4 to 56. In 1898 John Merrick founded a major black insurance company, North Carolina Mutual, and in 1905 Alonzo F. Herndon set up another substantial insurance provider for blacks, Atlanta Life Mutual. At the turn of the century, the largest black enterprise in New York City was a real estate brokerage that employed more than 200 people.

Many black companies were run as cooperatives, businesses owned by their employees. In 1906, Philadelphia boasted 10 black lending cooperatives that offered housing loans. In other cities exclusion from white cemeteries led blacks to form cooperative companies to create black cemeteries.

Madam C. J. Walker, at the wheel of her luxury automobile in 1912, pilots her friends around Indianapolis, home of her thriving cosmetics empire. Born to emancipated Louisiana slaves in 1867, Walker became America's first black female millionaire.

One of the most colorful entrepreneurs of the period was Madam C. J. Walker. In 1905, after Walker began to lose her hair prematurely at the age of 38, she developed a revolutionary hair-care method. Called the "Walker System," it combined scalp preparation, application of lotions, and the use of heated iron combs. Selling products for the treatment door-to-door, touting them as the first tailored specifically for blacks' cosmetic and health needs, she enjoyed immediate and immense success. Soon she had built a network of 3,000 saleswomen and had expanded her inventory to include a wide variety of beauty products. Within a few years, she became the nation's first black female millionaire. Her extravagant lifestyle and gift for self-promotion made her one of the best-known black Americans of the early 20th century. But as much as she immersed herself in opulence, buying palatial

Dressed in their best and ready to face an uncertain future, a southern farm family arrives in Chicago in the early 1900s. Ever-expanding black urban populations led to improved education and eventually to the formation of a new American social phenomenon: the black middle class.

Members of an integrated bricklayers' union assemble for a group portrait in the early 1900s. Such unrestricted associations were rare in this period; most labor "brother-hoods" not only refused entry to blacks but threatened to strike if employers hired black workers.

homes in Manhattan and Irvington-on-Hudson, New York, she still contributed generously to the black community, donating money to dozens of black charities, establishing college scholarships for black women, and rewarding her employees with bonuses and prizes.

Such economic success stories generally came in the face of enormous obstacles. Black entrepreneurs frequently found themselves targeted for acts of van-

dalism by their white competitors. Black artisans saw their customers increasingly desert them during the 1890s. And blacks working in southern industry encountered a double dose of discrimination, coming both from employers and labor unions. Many southern craft unions prohibited apprenticeships by blacks and many southern industrial unions went on strike to prevent employers from hiring blacks. In this manner, blacks were effectively excluded from the most lucrative component of the southern economy, textile manufacturing. In textiles, workers earned five times the average salary of black workers in other industries. Ultimately, only a minority of blacks were able to improve themselves economically around the turn of the century. In 1900, the majority of the nation's blacks still lived in poverty in rural areas.

In coping with poverty many blacks continued to seek refuge in the church, as they had for several decades. But black religious life underwent important changes around the turn of the century. For one thing, many educated blacks withdrew from the two standard black denominations, Baptist and Methodist, because they found their use of the Bible too literal and simplistic; instead, many joined Congregational, Presbyterian, Episcopal, and Catholic churches. At the same time, black churches began spending less time talking about the promises of the next world and more dealing with the problems of this world. Black churches increasingly offered social welfare services, such as employment bureaus, training programs for domestic workers, daycare centers, gymnasiums, homes for the aged and orphaned, and clubs for boys and girls.

In providing blacks with social services and a sense of community, churches were supplemented by black mutual aid associations and fraternal orders, which had sprung up in the South during the late 19th century. Mutual aid associations gave their members financial support in the event of sickness or death of family members. Some—such as the Young Mutual Society of Augusta, Georgia—were locally organized, and others encompassed a whole state—such as the Works Mutual Aid Association of Virginia, which claimed 4,000 members in 1900.

Black fraternal orders also furnished members with life insurance, but they differed from mutual aid groups in that they usually operated in secret, held social gatherings, and often invested their members' money. The Grand Fountain of the United Order of the Reformers, for example, which existed from 1881 to 1911, owned a bank, five department stores, and a weekly newspaper. The largest fraternal order was the Odd Fellows, which by 1906 included 4,000 lodges and held investments worth $3 million. Mutual aid associations and fraternal orders occasionally evolved into conventional business enterprises. For example, John Merrick's North Carolina Mutual Life Insurance Company grew out of a mutual aid group. And the bulk of black banks began their existence as depositories for fraternal orders.

Another response to economic hardship was a surge in migration by southern blacks to northern cities. In the words of historian John Hope Franklin, "The trickle of blacks northward that began in the late 1870s was almost a steady stream by 1900." Blacks were drawn by the possibility of finding employment in factories in northern cities, and in many cases were recruited by agents of northern industrial firms. Migrants from coastal states tended to chose northeastern cities as their destination, whereas migrants from the Middle South—Alabama, Mississippi, and Louisiana—usually ended up in such midwestern metropolises as Chicago, Detroit, and Cleveland. The flow of migrants at the turn of the century was small compared to the massive exodus that occurred between 1910 and 1945, the so-called Great Migration, which involved more than 3 million blacks. But the tens of thousands of blacks who ventured north between 1890 and 1910 established pathways and communities that eased the passage for later migrants.

5

NEW CULTURAL FRONTIERS

THE 20th century opened with an explosion of change—social, economic, and cultural—for African Americans. Each area stimulated the next; improved black education, for example, enlarged the black role on the American literary scene by providing literary training for potential writers and, at the same time, expanding the audience for books by those writers.

During the late 1890s, two of the first major African American writers emerged. (Until that time, the black contribution to American literature had been minimal because of low literacy levels and the strength of the oral tradition among blacks.) One of the first of these new creative forces was the nationally recognized poet Paul Laurence Dunbar. The son of former slaves, Dunbar was born in 1872 in Dayton, Ohio, where his parents had moved to escape Jim Crow. His poetic gifts revealed themselves throughout his childhood; he completed his first poem at the age of six, gave a public recital of his work at 13, and was

Sheet music from the hit Broadway show of 1906, Bandana Land, *features portraits of two of the era's most successful black showmen: Will Marion Cook (left) and Bert A. Williams (right). Recalling the opening of his 1898 smash,* Clorindy, the Origin of the Cakewalk, *Cook said, "Negroes were at last on Broadway, and there to stay. . . . Nothing could stop us."*

named class poet his senior year at Dayton's Central High School. The only black at Central, he also served as president of the literary society and editor of the school newspaper.

In spite of Dunbar's accomplishments, he did not attend college because he had to work to support his family. Finding it impossible to get work in his preferred fields —journalism and office work—he took a job as an elevator operator. He continued to turn out poems, published his first collection, *Oak and Ivy*, with his own funds in 1892, and sold the book to people who rode his elevator.

Dunbar's audience remained small until 1896, when a second self-published edition, *Majors and Minors*, caught the attention of the nation's preeminent man of letters, the novelist and critic William Dean Howells. Writing in *Harper's Weekly*, Howells gave the collection a glowing review, celebrating it as the first authentic representation of black life. He characterized it as a good example of literary realism, a school of writing of which Howells was then the foremost exponent. Written in black dialect—a form never before considered appropriate for poetry—Dunbar's poems depicted the lives of slaves and their masters in the pre–Civil War South.

In the years since Dunbar's first publications, his poetry has elicited a mixed critical response. Some scholars have faulted it for too closely following the example of fiction written by whites who aimed at romanticizing the Old South with the use of "darky" language. Others have accused Dunbar of perpetuating negative stereotypes about black people and black language. Historian Thomas Holt, for example, has dismissed Dunbar as "the literary equivalent of Booker T. Washington." Others, however, have found much humor and pathos in the poems. John Hope Franklin writes of Dunbar, "Few poets in America had been able to capture so completely the spirit of some aspect

of American life and to distill it into such delightful verse."

In any case, after Howells's review Dunbar became immensely popular with his contemporaries. In 1896, a major publishing house brought out a collection that included new poems and a selection from his previous two books. Called *Lyrics of Lowly Life*, it found a wide readership among both blacks and whites. Dunbar

Paul Laurence Dunbar, America's first nationally recognized black poet, moved into the spotlight with the publication of his second poetry collection, Majors and Minors, *in 1895.*

became a regular on the lecture circuit and went on to publish nine more books of verse. In addition, he wrote four short-story collections and four novels, one of which concerned a black family in Harlem and three of which, surprisingly enough, were melodramas involving wealthy white characters. But literary critics considered his fiction inferior to his poetry. In spite of his success, Dunbar was a troubled man—the result, some have speculated, of feeling artistically restrained by prevailing tastes. He began to drink heavily, and his alcoholism, along with tuberculosis, caused his premature death at the age of 34 in 1906.

Just as Dunbar was emerging as the first widely known black poet, Charles Chesnutt was establishing himself as the first celebrated black fiction writer. Chesnutt differed from Dunbar in that he did not gain recognition until relatively late in life—he was in his forties—after working as a teacher, principal, gossip columnist, legal stenographer, and lawyer. But in several other ways, the two were similar. Like Dunbar, Chesnutt was born in Ohio (in 1858), was the son of slaves, received assistance from William Dean Howells, and often wrote in dialect.

Also like Dunbar, Chesnutt has been criticized in subsequent years for allegedly writing about blacks in stereotyped language and echoing Washington's accommodationist views. Writers of the Harlem Renaissance in the 1920s were especially impatient with Chesnutt's moderate stance on race relations. On balance, however, scholars have looked more favorably on Chesnutt than Dunbar. The consensus seems to be that, whereas Dunbar used dialect to create a romanticized view of plantations before the Civil War, Chesnutt used dialect to create an original and realistic picture of black life during the rise of Jim Crow. Chesnutt also addressed the serious problems faced by black people, although he never attacked white supremacy in a militant way.

Charles W. Chesnutt, like Dunbar a pioneer of black American literature, and like Dunbar the son of former slaves, was—unlike Dunbar— the author of a number of provocative works addressing whites' injustice to blacks. He is best known for his 1900 novel, The House Behind the Cedars.

Chesnutt's first book, *The Conjure Woman,* published in 1899, was his least provocative; it consisted of a connected series of short stories about the Old South told in dialect by an old black gardener. His first novel, *The House Behind the Cedars,* published in 1900, was more daring. It traced the life of a light-skinned black character named Rena Walden. In an indirect way, it criticized white oppression of blacks by having Rena seek to "pass" as white in order to escape the difficult life blacks in her town endured. But it was also a classic melodrama: Rena's plans to marry her white suitor are foiled when her black heritage is discovered, and she

A quintet of performers
demonstrates the cakewalk, a
wildly popular dance that
featured high-stepping, prancing,
and strutting. Originating
among slaves of the early 19th
century, the cakewalk probably
started as a parody of white
people, whose movements slaves
saw as amusingly stilted.

dies a sudden death before her lover has a chance
to tell her he has had a change of heart.
Chesnutt's other two novels took on the

subject of racial conflict more directly. In *The Marrow of Tradition* (1901) he presented a harrowing picture of white attacks against blacks

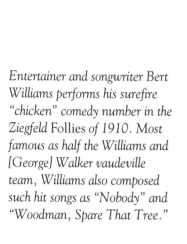

Entertainer and songwriter Bert Williams performs his surefire "chicken" comedy number in the Ziegfeld Follies of 1910. Most famous as half the Williams and [George] Walker vaudeville team, Williams also composed such hit songs as "Nobody" and "Woodman, Spare That Tree."

during the 1898 Wilmington race riot. But he softened his critique of white-on-black violence by having his sympathetic protagonist, a respected black doctor, advise blacks not to retaliate against whites. Similarly, in *The Colonel's Dream* (1905) he tempered his condemnation of the exploitation of black labor by giving a white character credit for devising a smart solution to such exploitation. Black writers were also turning out an increasing number of nonfiction works around the turn of the century. Chesnutt, in addition to his fiction, published a young people's biography of the great abolitionist leader Frederick Douglass in 1899.

Perhaps the most prolific author of nonfiction during the period, despite his many other commitments, was Booker T. Washington, who wrote books on black education, black business, and black history and produced the most celebrated autobiography of the time, *Up from Slavery*, published in 1900. A classic American story of a poor man rising to great power and wealth, and the most comprehensive statement of Washington's philosophy, the autobiography is still widely read today.

The proliferation of black periodicals gave black writers more places to publish their shorter pieces. By 1900 there were 150 black weekly newspapers, 3 black dailies, and 2 magazines: the *Southern Workman* and the *AME Review*.

Blacks, led by Will Marion Cook, also made breakthroughs in the theater at this time. A musical prodigy who was born in Washington, D.C., in 1869, Cook was accepted as a student by the nation's premier music school, Oberlin Conservatory, when he was only 13 years old, and later studied violin with classical composer Antonín Dvorák.

Cook made theatrical history when his musical, *Clorindy, the Origin of the Cakewalk*, opened at New York City's Casino Roof Garden in 1898. It was the first Broadway show to be composed or directed by a black person; it was also New York theatergoers' introduction to syncopated ragtime music. Featuring lyrics by Paul Laurence Dunbar, the one-act presentation consisted of comic sketches and dance numbers performed by black couples. Much of the show's style came out of the minstrel show tradition. (Stage entertainments featuring comic dialogues, song, and dance, minstrel shows were traditionally performed by white actors. Appearing in outrageous "blackface" makeup, they played either grinning, carefree slaves or crafty, conniving free blacks. After the Civil War, these shows began to include genuine blacks in black roles.)

Clorindy was a minstrel show shorn of its ugliest traits and transformed into simple musical comedy. A huge success, it played in New York for months, then traveled to most of the large cities on the East Coast.

At about the same time two black performers, Bert Williams and George Walker, became hugely popular with Americans of all races. Williams and Walker combined comedy, dance, and song in shows that, like Cook's, drew from the

Faced with America's monumental prejudice against black artists, Pittsburgh-born Henry Ossawa Tanner moved to Paris in 1891. There, the 32-year-old painter began to perfect the glowing naturalistic style that would win him a glittering international reputation and innumerable prizes.

minstrel show tradition. The performers, who began their careers in the honky-tonk barrooms of San Francisco, moved to New York in 1896. There they enjoyed great success with their show *The Song of Ham,* in which Walker portrayed a light-skinned dandy and Williams, in blackface, played a buffoonish dark-skinned black. The show opened in 1900 and ran for more than two years.

In 1902, Williams and Walker joined forces with Cook and Dunbar to create a major Broadway hit called *In Dahomey,* a musical farce about blacks moving back to Africa. The show was so well-received that its backers took it on the road, presenting it in London in 1903, where rave reviews prompted Edward VII, king of England, to insist on a private performance at Buckingham Palace.

Like Dunbar and Chesnutt, blacks working in the theater at the turn of the century have since been criticized for working in a genre that presented insulting images of blacks. But their shows, while they sometimes included demeaning stereotypes of blacks, also included a great deal of sharp comedy and creative music and dancing; they also opened up career opportunities for black directors, composers, and actors.

Painting was a less common mode of expression for blacks at the turn of the century. Nevertheless, one black painter, Henry Ossawa Tanner, won acclaim in both the United States and Europe. In doing so, he overcame enormous obstacles. As his dealer for many years, Erwin Barrie, later commented:

> For a Negro to achieve what he did at that time was incredible. It required great humility and even greater courage. He was a tenacious man. He conquered in spite of racial prejudice that was monumental.

Young W. C. Handy, seen here with the cornet he played in a marching band in the 1890s, became the first composer to recognize the importance of the blues, a musical form rooted in black folk experience. Composer of many well-known songs, including "St. Louis Blues" and "Careless Love," Handy is known as the Father of the Blues.

Born in Pennsylvania in 1859, Tanner wanted to develop his natural gifts as a painter, but he had trouble finding anyone to train him. During his teens, when he sought private lessons, he was rejected by teacher after teacher solely because of his race. Finally accepted at the Pennsylvania Academy of Fine Arts, he was often tormented by white students. For his "having asserted himself too much," for example, they once tied him to his easel and left him in the middle of a busy Philadelphia street. More supportive, however, were the academy's teachers, especially Thomas Eakins, one of the 19th century's most important American painters. Tanner was heavily influenced by Eakins and, early in his career, followed Eakins's lead in painting realistic landscapes and "psychological" portraits.

But Tanner's career really took off after he moved to Paris in 1891 and began to develop his own distinctive style: mystical religious painting with striking colors, radiant light, rich symbolism, and great depth of feeling. Unlike his black contemporaries involved in literature and theater, Tanner worked outside the dominant traditions, following his own idiosyncratic path. While most artists at the time practiced realism or impressionism, Tanner produced glowing religious canvases that harked back to the Renaissance. It was a lonely path that Tanner took—he was isolated by his race as well as his artistic style—but it was a rewarding one, both for him and for American culture.

In 1897, Tanner's painting *Raising of Lazarus* created a stir at the Paris Salon des Artistes and was purchased by the French government. Soon thereafter, Tanner won a string of awards that solidified his reputation not only as the most important black American artist to that date but as one of the most important American artists of any race. He received medals at the Paris Exposition of 1900, the Pan-American Exposition of 1901, and the St. Louis Exposition of 1904. In 1906, the French government purchased another Tanner work, *Disciples at Emmaus*, for its Luxembourg Museum; only two other American artists, James McNeill Whistler and John Singer Sargent, had ever earned that honor. In later years, many other famous museums—including the Louvre, the Metropolitan Museum of Art in New York, and the Los Angeles County Museum—obtained works by Tanner.

Black musicians of the period also bucked tradition, creating three new styles of music, all of which remain today among the most original and important forms of American music. Ragtime appeared around 1895. It took the standard half-note rhythm of minstrel-show music and syncopated it an infinite variety of ways. Unlike jazz and blues songs, ragtime pieces were composed rather than improvised. They consisted of several melodic themes stated, repeated, and alternated in various patterns.

Ragtime evolved in different places at the same time, but its foremost composer was Scott Joplin. Born in Texarkana, Texas, in 1868, Joplin received free piano lessons from a local German music teacher when he was a child and then refined his skills working in saloons along the Mississippi River. In 1899, he published his first major ragtime work, "Maple Leaf Rag." It brought him enough money to enable him to quit playing in bars, move to St. Louis, and get married. During the next 18 years, he wrote dozens of other ragtime songs as well as a few ragtime operas. He never fulfilled his dream, however, of persuading the country to accept ragtime as a serious, "classical" form of music. After he died in 1917, he was largely forgotten until the 1970s, when a new record of his songs sparked a revival of interest in ragtime. His compositions were featured in the 1973 movie *The Sting*, helped inspire a best-selling novel by E. L. Doctorow called *Ragtime*, and earned Joplin a posthumous Pulitzer Prize in 1976.

Also around the turn of the century, black musicians were refining the blues, a musical style that originated in slave songs. Initially a vocal form, the blues was taken up around the turn of the century by instrumentalists, and at the same time changed from a loose pattern to a fairly standard one: the 12-bar blues. In the 12-bar blues, each chorus includes 12 measures built around three chords (dominant, subdominant, and tonic), and each consists of three lines of lyrics, the second a repetition of the first, and the

third a variation. This standardization of the blues
made it more adaptable for popular songs. But it still
remained an unwritten, improvised music until 1912,
when W. C. Handy published the first composition,
"The Memphis Blues."

**When blues and ragtime came together in
these years, they helped produce jazz. Like ragtime, jazz materialized in several places at once,
but the most important was New Orleans. There
marching bands were a staple of daily life, playing
at parades, picnics, and funerals. One of the
marching bands, organized by Charles "Buddy"
Bolden, also played for parties. In this incarna-
tion, it created the first form of jazz, which
blended European instrumentation and melodies,
the syncopation of ragtime, and the structure and
improvisation of the blues.**

Beginning in the late 1890s, Buddy Bolden's band
played regularly in Storyville, New Orleans's red-light
district. The band comprised a cornet, played by
Bolden himself, a clarinet, a trombone, a banjo, and
drums. The horn players, called the "front line," took
turns playing themes and improvising on them, while
the banjo and drums, the "rhythm section," provided
percussion and harmony. Buddy Bolden died in 1907,
but the band played on, with the trombonist Frank
Dusen as the leader. Gradually, other Storyville
bands—black, white, Creole—began imitating the
Bolden style. Within a few years bands that played on
Mississippi riverboats had carried the music to Chicago, St. Louis, and several other cities.

6

TOWARD NIAGARA

AS the new century dawned, Booker T. Washington remained the most powerful black person in the United States. And his influence in national politics increased further after September 1901, when Theodore Roosevelt became president following the assassination of President William McKinley. Roosevelt unofficially made Washington his chief adviser on black affairs. Washington was unsuccessful in his secret attempt to use his access to Roosevelt to push for federal action against lynching and black disfranchisement.

But Roosevelt did regularly defer to Washington's wishes on political appointments. This was a mixed blessing for blacks. On the one hand, Washington opened up a host of new government positions for blacks. On the other hand, most of those positions

Key members of the Niagara Movement, formed to oppose Booker T. Washington's accommodationist policies, meet in Boston, Massachusetts in 1907. The movement was founded by activist scholar W. E. B. Du Bois (seated, left), who said, "We will fight for all time against any proposal to educate black boys and girls simply as servants and underlings, or simply for the use of other people."

A doctored picture—half photograph, half drawing— depicts a White House dinner that had all America talking. Black leaders applauded President Theodore Roosevelt's 1901 invitation to Booker T. Washington, but most whites, especially southerners, were shocked by the idea of a black man dining with the president.

were filled by his loyal lieutenants, who parroted his accommodationist views. Washington used his leverage over political appointments to reward supporters for their loyalty, building a patronage system compa-

rable to that employed by urban political bosses of the period.

On occasion Washington also used his control over appointments to rein in opposition. For example,

William H. Lewis, a black lawyer who graduated from Harvard Law School, had long been an outspoken critic of Washington when the Roosevelt administration began considering him for a Justice Department post. Lewis had Roosevelt's backing because the president admired Lewis's exploits as an all-American football player, but to get hired he needed Washington's blessing, too. Lewis made a deal with Washington, agreeing to curtail his disparagement of the Tuskegee leader in exchange for a position as U.S. district attorney in Boston. Only a few years later, under President William H. Taft, Lewis became assistant attorney general of the United States, the highest position in the executive branch occupied by a black to that point. Other blacks sponsored by Washington who received powerful slots included Robert Terrell, judge of the Washington municipal court from 1901 to 1921, and Charles Anderson, collector of internal revenue in New York from 1905 to 1915.

On October 16, 1901, Roosevelt demonstrated his respect for Washington by taking the controversial step of inviting him to dinner at the White House. Southern white leaders were incensed, believing that it was a horrible breach of etiquette for the nation's leader to share his table with a black person. An editorial in the white-owned *Richmond Dispatch*, for example, condemned the encounter by stating, "With our long-matured views on the subject of social intercourse between blacks and whites, the least we can say now is that we deplore the president's taste and we distrust his wisdom." Blacks, by contrast, applauded the meeting, interpreting it as meaning that Roosevelt favored black equality.

Ultimately, however, Roosevelt charted a wavering course on race relations that fully satisfied neither side. Blacks were elated and whites dismayed in 1903 when Roosevelt named a black man, William Crum, as collector of the port of Charleston, South Carolina, in defiance of a loud campaign against the appointment by white politicians. One black publication, the *Colored American Magazine*, called the appointment the "greatest political triumph in 20 years" for blacks. Roosevelt also endeared himself to blacks by refusing to give in to the demands of white citizens of Indianola, Mississippi, that he dismiss the black postmistress there. Then again, on other occasions Roosevelt flattered southern whites by praising their traditions and echoing their spurious claim that most lynchings were aimed at punishing black men who raped white women. Roosevelt felt he needed to say these things to maintain the support of southern white members of his party.

Clearly, the nation's chief executive was not the savior blacks had hoped for. In part because of growing realization of this fact, the first years of the 20th century brought increasing signs of impatience with Booker T. Washington's go-slow approach. One of the first signs of change was the appearance in Congress of a strict antilynching bill. Intended to make lynching a federal crime, the measure was introduced by George White of North Carolina, at the time the sole black member of Congress. It failed to pass, however, because southern whites enjoyed disproportionate influence in Congress. (They did so because of the Democratic party's monopoly in southern politics, which enabled southern Democrats in Congress to retain their seats for long periods of time and thereby build up the seniority needed to control committee memberships.)

Later that year, White lost his seat. He delivered a heartfelt farewell address on March 4, 1901, in which he vehemently condemned whites' treatment of blacks in the South. He characterized blacks as "an outraged, heartbroken, bruised and bleeding, but God-fearing people, faithful, industrious, loyal people—rising people, full of force." And he expressed confidence that blacks would return to Congress. It would, however, be 28 years before another black was elected to Congress.

Around the same time that opposition to accommodation disappeared from Congress with the departure of George White, a small group of elite blacks in the North began to speak out against Washington. Mostly editors, lawyers, ministers, and teachers, they were known as Radicals. The first to make his voice widely heard was a newspaperman, William Monroe Trotter. After obtaining his B.A. and M.A. from Harvard University, Trotter had worked for several years as an insurance and mortgage broker and made a great deal of money. But he forsook that career because, he said, "the conviction grew upon me that pursuit of happiness, money, civic, or literary position was like building a house upon sand; if race prejudice and persecution and public discrimination for mere color was to spread up from the South and result in a fixed caste of color, every colored American would be really a civil outcast, forever an alien in the public life."

In 1901, Trotter established a black newspaper in Boston called the *Guardian* as a forum in which to make his case against Washingtonian conciliation. He set up shop in the former offices of William Lloyd Garrison's *Liberator*, the foremost periodical of the

William Monroe Trotter, fiery publisher of the black Boston newspaper, the Guardian, savagely criticized Washington and his conciliatory approach to race relations. After Trotter launched a particularly heated attack on his opponent at a 1903 public meeting, Washington flexed his powerful political muscle—and Trotter served a monthlong jail sentence for "disorderly conduct."

abolitionist movement, as a way of linking himself in the minds of blacks with that revered movement. Trotter's attacks on Washington were not only ideological but personal as well. He invented a series of negative nicknames for Washington: the Benedict Arnold of the Negro Race, the Great Traitor, the Great Divider, the Exploiter of Exploiters, the Black Boss, and Pope Washington. He had unkind words even for Washington's personal appearance:

His features were harsh in the extreme. His vast leo-
nine jaw into which vast mastiff-like rows of teeth were
set clinched together like a vise. His forehead shot up to a
great cone; his chin was massive and square; his eyes were
dull and absolutely characterless, and with a glance that
would leave you uneasy and restless during the night if you
failed to report to the police such a man around before you
went to bed.

In 1903, Trotter broadened his campaign against
Washington, supplementing his editorial attacks with
an attempt to change the direction of the Afro-
American Council, the black organization revamped
by Ida Wells-Barnett in 1898. Since 1900, the group
had gradually moved away from Wells's militant point
of view. At its July 1903 meeting Trotter and his
associates tried to reverse this shift. Washington,
however, had too many allies on the council and was
able to fend off this power play.

Realizing that he could not pursue the Radical
agenda through existing institutions, Trotter opted
for less conventional means: he decided to stage a
public confrontation with Washington. His goal was
to dispel the widespread misconception that all blacks
supported accommodation, an illusion that Washington did his best to perpetuate, using his power to
screen media coverage of black affairs. On July 30,
1903, as Washington gave a speech at Boston's Zion
Church, Trotter stood up on a chair and delivered a
critique of Washington's philosophy in the form of
nine questions.

Trotter asked, for example, "When you said, 'It was
not so important whether the Negro was in the inferior car as whether there was in that car a superior man
not a beast,' did you not minimize the outrage of the
insulting Jim Crow car discrimination and justify it by
the bestiality of the Negro?" His last question packed
the strongest blow: "Are the rope and the torch all the
race is to get under your leadership?"

The police hustled Trotter out of the church and
arrested him for disorderly conduct. But he had

achieved his objective: the next day, newspapers devoted extensive coverage to what they called the
"Boston Riot." Americans had been given dramatic
evidence of dissent in the black community. The
incident also widened the rift between the Radicals
and Washington, whose response was typical; while
publicly he ignored the incident, privately he exerted
so much pressure on law enforcement officials that
Trotter was sentenced to a month in jail for his
behavior at the meeting. Trotter fought back with a
libel suit against Washington. But probably the most
significant consequence of the incident was that it
helped bring into the anti-Washington camp the
person who became its most articulate spokesman,
W. E. B. Du Bois.

Like Trotter, Du Bois was a northeastern intellectual with an Ivy League education. But whereas Trotter was a journalist, Du Bois was an academic. In 1895,
he had become the first black to receive a Ph.D. from
Harvard, and in 1896 he published his dissertation,
Suppression of the Slave Trade, a pathbreaking work on
the history of slavery. Several years earlier, while still
an undergraduate, he had begun to think of himself as
a leader of the black race. He believed that he and
other college-educated blacks had a special obligation
to represent the interests of everyday people; they
were, he said, "destined leaders of a noble people."

After becoming a college professor at Atlanta University in 1898, Du Bois attempted to fulfill this sense
of obligation by accumulating as much data as he
could on the mistreatment of blacks over the course
of American history. He thought that scholarly investigation of the oppression of blacks would help bring
about social reform. Every year he hosted an annual
conference of academics in Atlanta to discuss black
problems. And in 1899 he published *The Philadelphia
Negro*, the first comprehensive case study of an
American black community.

At this point in his career, Du Bois did not see any

need for militancy or agitation; exposure of injustice, he thought, would be enough. In fact, he was sympathetic to many of Booker T. Washington's ideas. For a time he even approved of such voting restrictions as poll taxes and literacy tests, reasoning that they would galvanize blacks to better themselves. In 1890, he had weighed in against a federal bill that would have prohibited some of the restrictions. Many blacks were "not fit for the responsibility of republican government," he argued, adding, "When you have the right sort of black voters you will need no election laws." Du Bois also shared Washington's interest in encouraging black self-help and promoting black entrepreneurship.

But as the 20th century began and Du Bois noticed that his scholarship was having little impact on social reform and that Washington's policies seemed to be inviting oppression, he changed his position. In articles published in the *Atlantic Monthly* and other periodicals, he began to criticize Washington. At first his objections were directed mainly at Washington's educational philosophy. He faulted the Tuskegee leader's program of industrial education as too materialistic, too concerned with teaching moneymaking skills, and not enough concerned with intellectual and spiritual development. He denigrated Washington for preaching a "gospel of work and money to such an extent as apparently almost completely to overshadow the higher aims of life."

In another essay Du Bois wrote, "If we make money the object of man-training, we shall develop money-makers, but not necessarily men; if we make technical skill the object of education, we may possess artisans but not, in nature, men." And Du Bois felt his view was shared by many other blacks: "We shall hardly induce black men to believe that if their stomachs are full, it matters little about their brains." To develop complete individuals, Du Bois held, vocational training had to be supplemented by instruction in liberal arts. Classes in history, sociology, literature, and other liberal arts were especially important in Du Bois's view for preparing talented blacks, whom Du Bois termed the "talented tenth," to become race leaders. It was this talented tenth, Du Bois maintained, who would lead blacks out of economic and cultural privation.

Gradually Du Bois widened his criticism to encompass Washington's whole program of conciliation. He decided that Washington had it backward when he insisted that black economic progress would eventually bring full political rights. On the contrary, Du Bois asserted, without political rights black success in the economic realm would always be precarious and black entrepreneurs vulnerable to interference by whites.

As evidence of the failure of Washington's methods, Du Bois called attention to the increase of segregation and disfranchisement laws since accommodation became the norm. It particularly galled Du Bois that Washington, instead of just ignoring white supremacists, flattered and paid court to them and echoed their contention that blacks were to blame for their own problems. Even if Washington intended these gestures as tactical maneuvers, as temporary compromises, Du Bois believed they increased the likelihood of a permanent caste system with blacks at the bottom; Washington, he said, had made a compromise that "practically accepted the alleged inferiority of the Negro." In order to obtain equal rights, Du Bois argued, blacks needed to stop currying favor

At first an admirer of
Washington, W. E. B.
Du Bois became
increasingly impatient with
what he called Washington's
"namby-pamby policy" of
accommodation. By shifting
"the burden of the Negro
problem to the Negro's
shoulders," said the disgusted
Du Bois in 1903, Washington
was actually "leading the
way backward."

with the architects of Jim Crow and instead protest
loudly against their subjugation. In a famous turn of
phrase, he concluded that "the problem of the twen-
tieth century is the problem of the color line."

Du Bois's attacks on Washington at first attracted
only moderate attention because they were expressed
in a wide assortment of articles that appeared in many
different publications. But in 1903, when the pieces
were collected and published in book form as *The Souls
of Black Folk*, they had a major impact. The writer
James Weldon Johnson later wrote that *The Souls of
Black Folk* had more influence on black readers than
any book except *Uncle Tom's Cabin*. The book gave
Du Bois the reputation as Washington's foremost

critic and attracted increased support to the Radical position. Soon afterward the "Boston Riot" occurred, and Du Bois was appalled by Washington's harsh retaliation against Trotter. Now Du Bois lashed out at Washington even more vociferously.

In January 1904, Du Bois and Washington made one last effort to resolve their differences, but it was a halfhearted one. At the urging of Andrew Carnegie, who favored unity among black leaders out of concern for black education, Du Bois and Washington agreed to meet along with 30 other prominent blacks at a secret gathering at New York's Carnegie Hall. From the beginning of the convention, however, both did their best to undermine the possibility of rapprochement. Washington sought to intimidate Du Bois supporters by packing the hall with his henchmen. For his part, Du Bois tried to persuade the assembly to condemn Washington. He believed that if Washington's delegates were presented with strong enough arguments against the policy of accommodation, they would turn on their leader. During the meeting Du Bois presented a list of demands that constituted his basic agenda for the next 30 years:

Full political rights on the same terms as other Americans
Higher education of selected Negro youth
Industrial education for the masses; common school training for every Negro child
A stoppage to the campaign of self-depreciation
A careful study of the real conditions of the Negro
A national Negro periodical
The raising of a defense fund
A judicious fight in the courts for civil rights

When the majority of delegates rejected the program, Du Bois resigned in protest. From that point on, he devoted himself to forming a formal black rights organization with all the individuals who supported protest. He traveled from city to city, soliciting the support of dozens of radicals. Through these efforts he brought about, in the words of James Weldon Johnson, "a coalescence of the more radical camps, thereby creating a split of the race into contending camps."

In July 1905, Du Bois assembled a collection of 29 of these radicals for three days of discussions in Niagara Falls. By the third day they had founded a black protest organization called the Niagara Movement. They were forced to meet on the Canadian side of the falls because no hotel on the American side would accept black customers—thus confirming for them the necessity of their meeting. In a series of resolutions, they made clear what the new organization stood for. Mostly written by Du Bois, the resolutions were intended to attract black supporters away from Washington and to stir the conscience of whites. They placed the blame for blacks' low status squarely on the shoulders of white supremacists. As one particularly stirring passage put it:

> The Negro race in America, stolen, ravished, and degraded, struggling up through difficulties and oppression, needs sympathy and receives criticism, needs help and is given hindrance, needs protection and is given mob-violence, needs justice and is given charity, needs leadership and is given cowardice and apology, needs bread and is given a stone.

Members of the organization committed themselves to fervent condemnation of oppression and urged other blacks to follow their lead. "We do not hesitate," they declared, "to complain and to complain loudly and insistently. To ignore, overlook, or apologize for these wrongs is

Smiling at his mostly white audience, Washington acknowledges applause after a speech at Tuskegee. Du Bois's criticism of his ingratiating style infuriated the Tuskegee chief: "It is difficult to see," he said bitterly, "how people can throw away their time and strength in stirring up strife within the race."

to prove ourselves unworthy of freedom. Persistent, manly agitation is the way to liberty."

In terms of more specific goals, the movement called for an end to segregation, racial violence, and the disfranchisement of blacks. But it also demanded equal access to education for blacks, equal economic opportunity, equal treatment in the courts, the elimination of all caste distinctions based on race, recognition of the basic principles of brotherhood, respect for the working man, and the "right of freemen to walk, talk, and be with them that wish to be with us."

Niagara members were also determined to break Washington's single-handed control over news about African Americans that appeared in the black and the white press. Hence, two of the group's other stated aims were "to oppose firmly the present method of strangling honest criticism, manipulating public opinion and centralizing political power" and "to establish and support major proper organs of news and public opinion." In addition to attacking Washington's methods, Niagara members made personal attacks. They called Washington a coward and a puppet of whites. And they referred to him as "half-educated," because he had attended an industrial school. They insisted that only graduates of liberal arts colleges like themselves were fit to lead the race.

The Niagara Movement represented the first African American institution dedicated exclusively to protesting racial oppression. The Afro-American Council had for a time, after its reorganization by Wells-Barnett, engaged in protest. But it had other reasons for existing—for example, to guide black education. And it always included in its ranks many Washington followers, who had wrested control of the group away from the Wells-Barnett camp only a few years after the 1898 shift toward militancy. Moreover, the council, unlike the Niagara Movement, never had local chapters to carry out its wishes at the local level.

During the 1905 meeting the Niagara founders decided to hold annual meetings in order to issue declarations of protest to white America. They tried to choose sites for the meetings that had symbolic importance. So in August 1906, they convened in Harper's Ferry, West Virginia, where in 1859 the abolitionist leader John Brown had led an unsuccessful uprising against slavery. Before beginning actual discussions, members conducted a march through the arsenal that Brown's men had seized; then they sang "The Battle Hymn of the Republic" at the engine house where Brown made his last stand before being captured, tried, and hanged.

This second meeting drew a larger crowd than the first: more than 100 delegates came. Liberal white journalist Mary White Ovington covered the meeting for the *New York Evening Post* and was deeply affected by it; thereafter she became heavily involved in civil rights activities. At the end of the meeting the movement issued an "Address to the Country," written by Du Bois in "a tumult of emotion," as he described it. The address concluded with these eloquent words:

> We will not be satisfied to take one jot or tittle less than our full manhood rights. We claim for ourselves every single right that belongs to a freeborn American, political, civil, and social; and until we get these rights we will never cease to protest and assail the ears of America. The battle we wage is not for ourselves alone but for all true Americans.

7

THE TROUBLES CONTINUE

N OT surprisingly, Booker T. Washington did not take kindly to the emergence of an organization that rejected his policy of accommodation. And he was not about to sit idly by while the Niagara Movement made inroads into his power base and threatened to rock the boat of race relations. Soon after the Niagara Movement's inaugural meeting, Washington initiated efforts to discredit its members and disrupt its activities, employing the same kind of tactics he had used to silence previous opponents.

Washington hired private investigators from the Pinkerton agency to seek out damaging information on Niagara members, assigning them, for example, to find out whether Du Bois paid his taxes and whether Trotter's wife had worked as a domestic. He also dispatched secret agents to infiltrate the Niagara leadership and to bribe black newspapers to ignore Niagara meetings. One of Washington's henchmen, Melvin Chisum, played a particularly active role in the espionage campaign. Chisum spied on Trotter in Boston,

Washington (at door of railroad car) surveys members of the so-called Tuskegee Machine, a network of supporters who rewarded his allies and sabotaged his enemies. Washington's lieutenants regarded him with both respect and fear; some even addressed him as "Your Eminence."

113

Women's Congress delegates—prominent black women from 25 states—assemble in Atlanta, Georgia, for the 1895 Cotton States and International Exposition. Such all-female groups gained increasing influence, especially within the African American community, around the turn of the century.

posed as a member of Niagara's Brooklyn branch, and paid a Washington, D.C., newspaper to squelch reports about the movement's progress.

In the end, sabotage was probably unnecessary. The Niagara Movement never posed much of a threat to the imposing Tuskegee Machine. In no point during its five-year existence did the movement come close to building a following to rival Washington's. The reasons were several: Niagara's reluctance to cultivate white allies, its failure to appeal to the black masses, and its insistence on ideological conformity among members. By contrast Washington, with his politician's instincts, welcomed support from anyone willing to give it, regardless of race, class, or political stance; unlike the intellectuals who formed Niagara, he refused to restrict his reach to the black elite.

The Niagara Movement produced few tangible changes. It did help resist school segregation in Chicago and Philadelphia, and it won a suit against a northern railroad company that forced the company to stop segregating its passenger cars. Otherwise, its concrete impact was minimal.

Niagara was important for other reasons, however. It built connections among blacks who had previously challenged Jim Crow individually. Thus it laid the groundwork for an organization that would bring about substantive progress. Moreover, although it gained the approval of only a small minority of blacks, that minority grew considerably over the course of its existence. Between 1905 and 1910 an increasing number of blacks came to back a strategy of ardent protest. By 1908 the movement had received the endorsement of the National Association of Colored Women, the Equal Suffrage League, and several other black institutions.

In July 1905, the cause of protest acquired a forceful new voice when Chicagoan Robert Abbott launched a black newspaper, the *Defender*. Abbott's paper pulled no punches in lashing out at the injustices of Jim Crow, and it quickly acquired a reputation as the most militant, and one of the most distinguished, black publications. Abbott was a somewhat unlikely candidate for militancy, considering that he had attended the same industrial school as Booker T. Washington—Hampton Institute—and studied under the same man who first interested Washington in economic self-help. Abbott was too sickened, however, by the brutal treatment of blacks in the South to be content with pursuing mere economic success.

Ultimately, Abbott's paper did bring him enormous success. Starting as a minor weekly staffed mostly by former servants and barbers, the *Defender* grew to become one of the largest black papers in the country, reaching a circulation of 200,000 in the 1940s. But this success mostly came as a by-product of the pursuit of equality. It is true that Abbott built his readership by introducing to black journalism the sensationalist techniques of "yellow" journalism, which had recently been perfected by white newspaper publishers William Randolph Hearst and Joseph Pulitzer. Lynchings were covered in lurid detail and with gory photographs. But Abbott also always made room in his tabloid for serious writing, featuring, for example, the early work of the noted black poet Gwendolyn Brooks.

In 1906, the Radicals gained a key ally in education when John Hope, who had recently been named the first black president of Atlanta Baptist College (now called Morehouse College), joined the Niagara Movement. In fact, Hope was the only black college president who dared challenge Booker T. Washington; in doing so, he risked having Washington use his influence with the northern white elite to cut off philanthropic aid to Atlanta Baptist.

Like Abbott, Hope traveled an unusual road to militancy. He came from a relatively privileged background, which had shielded him much of the time from the indignities of racial discrimination. His father was wealthy and white, a Scottish immigrant who made a fortune importing liquor. Hope inherited his father's blue eyes and blond hair, so he could pass for white when he wanted to. As an adult, Hope could remember only two times during his childhood when he was struck by the cruelty of Jim Crow: the first occurred when he witnessed brutal race riots in Hamburg, Georgia; the second happened when callous white executors cheated him out of part of his inheritance after his father died. Despite losing this money, Hope went on to receive a superior education, attending a prep school in Massachusetts and earning a B.A. and M.A. from Brown University. After graduation he quickly rose through the ranks of black academia. So, ultimately, he came to advocate protest less because of personal experience of oppression than because of sympathy toward the oppression of others.

A rising tide of racial conflicts after 1905 confirmed Hope and other Niagara members in their belief that blacks needed to stand up more determinedly for their rights.

In August 1906, black soldiers stationed in Brownsville, Texas, were involved in a bloody shootout. The soldiers, members of the all-black 25th Regiment, had been repeatedly called racist names by local whites. When they finally responded to this taunting with physical force, they were engaged by a group of armed local residents and police officers. In the ensuing battle three white men were killed. Brownsville whites were furious, insisting that the black soldiers were solely to blame for the incident; blacks had "shot up the town," they claimed.

An investigation by law enforcement authorities concurred with the local citizens, and as a result, in November President Roosevelt dismissed three entire companies of black soldiers without honor. Black leaders, believing that the whites who provoked the black soldiers should share the blame, saw Roosevelt's action as yet another sign that he could not be counted upon to represent black interests. Several U.S. senators, too, were disturbed that Roosevelt had discharged the soldiers without a full and fair trial. Led by Senator Joseph Foraker of Ohio, they convened a Senate subcommittee to conduct an inquiry, but it

White Atlantans attack blacks during the city's murderous riot of September 1906. Although 12 blacks died and dozens of others suffered injury in the violence, Washington's response was characteristically passive: Atlanta's blacks, he said, should "exercise self-control and not make the fatal mistake of attempting to retaliate."

also concluded that the soldiers were guilty. Not until 1972 were the dishonorable discharges finally reversed. By that time only one member of the companies remained alive, and he received only $25,000 for his trouble.

Later in 1906, one of the worst race riots in American history broke out in Atlanta. It was sparked by false reports in several irresponsible white newspapers that four attacks had been made on white women by black men. To avenge these fictional threats to their womenfolk, gangs of white Atlanta men took to the streets on September 22, 1906, assaulting blacks and torching their property. They were eagerly abetted by rural whites in town for weekend shopping.

Instead of seeking to quell the violence, the Atlanta police made it worse. They not only refused to

protect blacks from the angry mobs, they also dis-
armed blacks who tried to protect themselves, and in
some instances joined in the attacks. One officer, for
instance, when asked for assistance by the president
of a black seminary, pistol-whipped the man. The riot
went on for several days, bringing commerce in the
city to a standstill. By the time it ended, 12 blacks had
been killed and 70 injured. The skirmish did have one
positive outcome: it led to the formation of an interracial group called the Atlanta Civic League, which
sought to improve the lot of blacks in the city. But the
riot led many blacks to pick up and leave for the
North. And it severely strained relations between
black and white residents of the South's most important city.

As blacks began to migrate north in larger
numbers, some whites regarded them with hostility. Racial tensions spread like a bloodstain. In
August 1908 they engulfed Springfield, Illinois—Abraham Lincoln's onetime hometown—
in violence and terror. As in Atlanta, the
Springfield tragedy began with the alleged assault
of a white woman by a black man. In this case,
the woman told the police that a black man
named George Richardson had broken into her
home and raped her. Later testifying before a
grand jury, she admitted that her assailant had
been a white man and that she accused Richardson only because he happened to be working in
the neighborhood. But by this point an unruly
mob had gathered in the streets.

Attempting to put out the fire, local authorities spirited Richardson out of town and mobi-
lized the state militia. But their moves simply

Jack Johnson (right) confronts Tommy Burns in Sydney, Australia, on December 26, 1908. Johnson's defeat of the white fighter made him the first black heavyweight champion of the world, delighting blacks but triggering race riots in which at least eight blacks died.

fanned the flames: members of the mob now grabbed guns, axes, and clubs and started beating black citizens and ransacking their businesses and homes. In an especially grisly encounter, the mob burned down a barbershop and hanged its owner. His crime: having black skin. In full view of the state legislature's offices, whites lynched a helpless 84-year-old black man. His crime: 30 years of happy marriage to a white woman. More than 5,000 militiamen ended the riot at last, but no whites ever came to trial. Blacks found this extremely upsetting; not even the North, they now saw, offered protection against racist attacks.

Three months after the Springfield riot, blacks got more bad news with the November 1908 election of President William Howard Taft. While serving as secretary of war under Theodore Roosevelt, Taft had made clear that he sympathized more with southern whites than southern blacks: he had expressed approval of poll taxes and disapproval of higher education for blacks. As president, he surprised no one by showing little regard for African American interests, allowing segregation for the first time in some federal office buildings, and canceling the appointment of black officials who were opposed by southern whites.

A month after Taft's election, on December 26, 1908, blacks received some welcome relief from the seemingly endless round of bad news: Jack Johnson defeated world champion Tommy Burns in Sydney, Australia, thereby becoming the first black heavyweight champion of the world. A fifth-grade dropout, Johnson had risen from a life as a panhandler and drifter to capture the title. Today, he is regarded by some boxing experts as the best heavyweight ever. Nat Fleischer, who founded the nation's leading boxing publication, *Ring* magazine, in 1922, recently declared, for example, "I have no hesitation in naming Jack Johnson as the greatest of them all." But at the time whites felt threatened by his accomplishments.

After the Australia fight some whites set out to find a "great white hope" to dethrone Johnson. In 1910 the white boxer James J. Jeffries, a former champion, was coaxed out of retirement to fill this role. On July 4 of that year, however, he too fell to Johnson, in Reno, Nevada. Blacks greeted Johnson's victory with delight, but it infuriated white racists, and fights took place across the country. Most of them starting when angry Jeffries fans attacked jubilant Johnsonists, these racial disturbances took at least eight black lives. Not until 1915 would Johnson lose his crown (to Jess Willard, in the 26th round). He would end his career with 107 wins and 6 losses.

8

THE BIRTH OF THE NAACP

THE bloody race riots of 1906 and 1908 triggered a storm of verbal protest from the Niagara Movement. In a powerful essay, "Address to the World," W. E. B. Du Bois blasted President Roosevelt for dismissing the black soldiers in Brownsville; after the 1908 Springfield riot, the movement publicly "cursed" those they identified as the "Negro haters of America." But Niagara's only weapons were words. Feeling increasingly impotent, its members became frustrated and demoralized, and many stopped paying their dues. The movement was damaged further by factional disputes. At the 1907 meeting, held in Boston because of the city's historic role as a center of abolitionism, Du Bois and William Monroe Trotter had a serious disagreement; Trotter reacted by abandoning the movement. By 1908 Du Bois realized that Niagara was losing power. The group held annual meetings through 1910, but for its last two years it merely limped along.

Niagara was disintegrating, but the Springfield riot

W. E. B. Du Bois (second from the right) checks copy at the office of the Crisis, *the newspaper he edited for the National Association for the Advancement of Colored People (NAACP). First appearing in November 1910, the* Crisis *stood, said Du Bois, "for the rights of men, irrespective of color or race."*

Mary White Ovington, the first white social worker to live and work in New York City's black ghetto, organized a biracial discussion group after she read William E. Walling's article about the 1908 Springfield riot. That group soon expanded into the NAACP, America's first effective civil rights organization.

had sparked another, more significant civil rights organization. That violent episode disturbed northern white liberals because it proved that racial conflicts were not confined to the South. Instrumental in stirring concern was a moving article about the riot, "Race War in the North," by journalist William English Walling. The piece, published in the *Independent*, described the gruesome events in vivid detail and hotly denounced the whites who had started the melee. It also included a stern warning to northern whites: if they did not act quickly to defend the rights of their black neighbors, Jim Crow would spread beyond the South. "Either the spirit of the abolitionists must be revived," Walling declared, "and we must come to treat the Negro on a plane of absolute political and social equality or [southern leaders] will have transferred the race war to the North." The article concluded with the plaintive question: "Who realizes the seriousness of the situation and what large and powerful body of citizens is ready to come to their aid?"

When Mary White Ovington, the white journalist and social worker who had covered the second meeting of the Niagara Movement, read the article, she was inspired to act. Together with Walling and Henry Moscowitz, another liberal social worker, she began arranging a conference to deal with racial discrimination. Oswald Garrison Villard, publisher of the *New York Evening Post* and grandson of noted abolitionist William Lloyd Garrison, agreed to help publicize the meeting, and he wrote the announcement. "We call," he wrote, "upon all believers in democracy to join in a national conference for the discussion of present evils, the voicing of protests, and the renewal of the struggle for civil and political liberty."

The meeting, called the National Negro Conference, was held in New York City on February 12, 1909, the 100th anniversary of Abraham Lincoln's birth. It attracted all the major figures from the Niagara Movement except Monroe Trotter, who declined to participate because, he said, he did not "trust white folks." Also in attendance were many prominent white liberals, including William Dean Howells, the writer who had promoted the careers of Charles Chesnutt and Paul Laurence Dunbar; Thomas Dewey, the era's most respected American educator and philosopher; and Jane Addams, the famed Chicago social worker who had founded Hull House.

In the discussions, delegates focused on the same issues as the Niagara Movement had. Du Bois and Ida Wells-Barnett spoke about the importance of securing the right of all blacks to vote. Others inveighed against segregation and mob violence and echoed Du Bois's desire to create rigorous academic programs for the most gifted blacks. All these issues were incorporated into a formal plan of action approved by the delegates. At the end of the meeting, they agreed to establish a permanent organization to carry out their plan.

Thus was born the nation's first major civil rights organization, the National Association for the Advancement of Colored People (NAACP). After the details had been worked out, it set up headquarters in New York City in May 1910 and went into operation. Villard, a skilled administrator, oversaw the transition with Ovington's assistance. Among the new organization's leaders were Moorfield Storey, a white lawyer from Boston with a long history of service in black causes, who was named the first president; Ovington, who was named secretary; and Walter Sachs, the first treasurer.

Du Bois was chosen head of research and publicity, a job that included editing the group's newspaper, the *Crisis*. He quit his post at Atlanta University, moved to New York, and brought out the first issue in November 1910. It contained a summary of the organization's position; it stood, he said, "for the rights of men, irrespective of color or race, for the highest ideals of American democracy, and for reasonable but earnest attempts to gain these rights and realize these ideals." In addition to its main office, the NAACP also opened numerous local branches.

The Niagara Movement continued to exist for several months after the NAACP came into being,

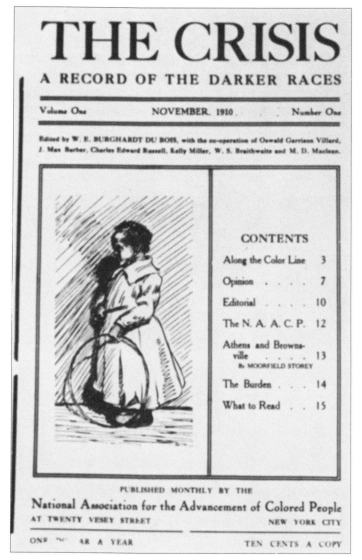

The first issue of the Crisis contained a Du Bois article entitled "Along the Color Line." The newspaper's success, recalled the editor, "was phenomenal. . . . With this organ of propaganda and defense we were able to organize one of the most effective assaults of liberalism upon reaction that the modern world has seen."

but most of its members joined the newer organization. The NAACP was in one sense Niagara's successor: it benefited from the enthusiasm for protest that Niagara had inspired, and it adopted Niagara's own goals.

The nation's white liberals boarded the NAACP bandwagon, but most of them also continued to sup-

Booker T. Washington harangues a Louisiana audience in 1915. The once all-powerful leader, who felt his authority slipping after the rise of the NAACP, became increasingly sharp in his opposition to Du Bois and others he regarded as enemies.

port Booker T. Washington and his conciliatory approach to black progress. At the same time, the organization included in its ranks the best and brightest black radical leaders, men and women such as Du Bois and Wells-Barnett (although she later broke with the group because she found it too moderate). And at the local level, most members of the branches—the organization's real backbone—were representatives of the college-educated black elite.

Booker T. Washington saw the NAACP as an even greater threat than the Niagara Movement; to cripple it, he used every form of pressure he knew. Just as he had earlier tried to damage Du Bois's and Trotter's reputations, after 1909 he targeted white liberal NAACP members for harassment. Rounding up a group of newspaper reporters loyal to his camp, he ordered them to dig up unsavory information about the liberals, even arranging for the reporters to sneak into meetings of the liberals' private social group, the Cosmopolitan Club. But the NAACP was far more resilient than the Niagara Movement had been, and it survived Washington's attacks with little effort. Its defense was strengthened by the decline in Washington's prestige, which had been somewhat tarnished by his lack of influence with President Roosevelt's successors, William Howard Taft and Woodrow Wilson. In addition, protest was growing increasingly respectable in the black community. Washington was to die in 1915; after that, his disciples would make peace with the NAACP.

From the beginning the NAACP was far more powerful and successful than its predecessor, partly because of its biracial character. The presence of white luminaries among the leadership helped attract financial backing and media attention that the Niagara Movement never enjoyed. The organization's biracial policy did, however, cause a few problems: except for Du Bois, all the top officials were white, a situation that fanned some resentment among the rank and file. The paternalistic attitude displayed by some white leaders also annoyed blacks. But as time went on, these internal racial tensions receded, eventually posing little problem.

Floating from the NAACP's offices on Manhattan's lower Fifth Avenue, a grim banner speaks for the organization's mission. NAACP leaders relentlessly pounded away on the white public's consciousness, making people aware of the horror of lynching and ultimately wiping it out as an American institution.

The NAACP cultivated its grass roots carefully. By 1914 it would boast 50 branches with some 6,000 members; by 1920 the number of branches would jump to 400. These offshoots were to prove invaluable for spreading information, raising funds, and conducting local campaigns against racial injustice. But the most important factor in the NAACP's success was its development of practical tactics. And of these, the strongest was legal action.

The group's Legal Redress Committee, headed by Arthur Spingarn, hired a team of top-notch black and white lawyers. This core group was supplemented by a part-time staff of volunteers that included such eminent attorneys as Clarence Darrow, Louis Marshall, and future Supreme Court justice Felix Frankfurter. By the end of the NAACP's first year its lawyers had won two important cases, one involving a Baltimore segregation statute, the other securing the release of two black New Jersey men wrongfully charged with murder.

Legal action was the NAACP's most potent weapon, but not its only one. Du Bois's scholarly, in-depth investigations of racial abuse also struck hard at Jim Crow, in part because they reached so many people. They owed their large audience to the impressive membership of the NAACP branches, to the ability of prominent whites on the board to attract attention, and to the *Crisis*, whose circulation would rise from 10,000 in its first year to 100,000 in its tenth.

The NAACP's aggressive publicity campaigns proved especially successful in combating lynching. The organization used essentially the same tactic that Wells-Barnett had, rallying public opinion against the crime by reporting each occurrence in grim detail. The NAACP was less effective, however, in its attempts to pass legislation; in the coming years NAACP officials would expend immeasurable effort lobbying for a federal antilynching law, but—even up to the present moment—no such measure ever cleared Congress.

Beginning in 1909 as a small, little-known clique of black radicals and white liberals, the NAACP would go on to play an instrumental role in reforming American social policy. Slowly chipping away at Jim

Crow, the organization would expose the evils of racial oppression, greatly reduce lynching, destroy the "grandfather clause" that illegally kept blacks from the South's polls, and get many residential segregation ordinances thrown out. In time, it would also engineer the demise of the "white primary" and of segregation in graduate schools.

When it emerged in 1909, the NAACP gave America's beleaguered black community a jolt of much-needed encouragement. The prior decade had been, in a number of ways, a nadir for blacks. The years between 1896 and 1909 witnessed a vast expansion of legal and de facto segregation across the South, the disfranchisement of the majority of southern blacks, and the outbreak of terrible racial violence in both the North and the South. Yet as oppressed and abused as African Americans were during this era, they could claim an array of significant achievements. They greatly improved educational opportunities for their children; set up scores of banks, insurance companies, and other successful businesses; created new fraternal societies; strengthened the black church; enlarged the black middle class; expanded black participation in northern and southern industry; and established pathways of migration to the North that would later serve as routes to economic opportunity. They also produced important works of literature and art, made valuable contributions to American theater, and pioneered three major new forms of music: ragtime, blues, and jazz.

Perhaps most important, the period saw the first stirrings of black protest. Although conciliation remained the dominant approach in 1909, an increasing number of blacks had made the courageous decision to resist Jim Crow—a process that began with Ida Wells's lonely crusade against lynching and culminated in the birth of the NAACP. Between 1896 and 1909 American blacks had begun to travel the difficult road from accommodation to resistance. In some respects a time of hate, these years also led to an era of hope.

FURTHER READING

Ayers, Edward L. *The Promise of the New South: Life After Reconstruction.* New York: Oxford University Press, 1992.

Bennett, Lerone, Jr. *Before the Mayflower: A History of Black America 1619–1964.* New York: Penguin, 1988.

Du Bois, W. E. B. *The Souls of Black Folk: Essays and Sketches.* 1903. Reprint. New York: Vintage Books/Library of America, 1990.

Fox, Stephen. *The Guardian of Boston: William Monroe Trotter.* New York: Atheneum, 1970.

Franklin, John Hope. *From Slavery to Freedom: A History of Negro Americans.* New York: Knopf, 1987.

Harlan, Louis. *Booker T. Washington: The Making of a Black Leader, 1856–1901.* New York: Oxford University Press, 1972.

———. *Booker T. Washington: The Wizard of Tuskegee, 1901–1915.* New York: Oxford University Press, 1983.

Harris, William H. *The Harder We Run: Black Workers Since the Civil War.* New York: Oxford University Press, 1982.

Hughes, Langston, Milton Meltzer, and C. Eric Lincoln. *A Pictorial History of Black Americans.* New York: Crown, 1983.

Kellogg, Charles Flint. *NAACP: A History of the National Association for the Advancement of Colored People.* Baltimore: Johns Hopkins Press, 1967.

Klots, Steve. *Ida Wells-Barnett.* New York: Chelsea House, 1993.

Lofgren, Charles. *The Plessy Case: A Legal-Historical Interpretation.* New York: Oxford University Press, 1987.

Marable, Manning. *W. E. B. Du Bois: Black Radical Democrat.* Boston: Twayne, 1986.

Ovington, Mary White. *The Walls Came Tumbling Down.* New York: Schocken, 1970.

Schroeder, Alan. *Booker T. Washington.* New York: Chelsea House, 1992.

Stafford, Mark. *W. E. B. Du Bois*. New York: Chelsea House, 1989.

Washington, Booker T. *My Larger Education*. Garden City, NY: Doubleday, 1911.

———. *Up from Slavery*. 1901. Reprint. New York: Viking Penguin, 1986.

Washington, E. Davidson, ed. *Selected Speeches of Booker T. Washington*. Garden City, NY: Doubleday, 1932.

Wells, Ida B. *Crusade for Justice: The Autobiography of Ida B. Wells*. Chicago: University of Chicago Press, 1970.

INDEX

PICTURE CREDITS

Archive Photos: pp. 16–17, 23 (American Stock), 28, 30–31(Lambert); Atlanta Historical Society: p. 118; The Bettmann Archive: pp. 24, 38, 52–53, 109; Collection of A'Lelia Bundles: p. 72; The University of Chicago Library: p. 43; Cleveland Public Library: p. 83; Department of Cultural Resources, North Carolina Division of Archives and History: pp. 56–57; Frank Driggs Collection: pp. 78–79, 90; Florida State Archives: pp. 19, 74–75; Library of Congress: pp. 40, 64–65, 68, 134; University of Massachusetts at Amherst: pp. 94–95, 124; Mississippi Valley Collection Libraries, Memphis State University, Memphis, TN: p. 114; Missouri Historical Society: p. 58; Courtesy of North Carolina Mutual Insurance Company: p. 70; Gary Phillips: p. 120; The Schomburg Center for Research in Black Culture, The New York Public Library, Astor, Lenox and Tilden Foundation: pp. 22, 47, 62, 73, 81, 84–85, 86, 88, 101, 106, 122–123, 127, 130; Smithsonian Institution, Washington, D.C.: pp. 96–97; Courtesy of Tuskegee Institute Archives, Tuskegee, AL: pp. 2, 32–33, 34–35, 48–49, 112–113, 128.

PIERRE HAUSER, a New York–based writer specializing in American history, has a B.A. in history from Yale, an M.A. in history from Columbia, and is currently a doctoral candidate in history at Columbia. He has worked as a book editor for a New York publishing firm, as a park ranger in the Southwest, and as a reporter for several San Francisco–area newspapers, including the Pulitzer Prize–winning *Point Reyes Light*. Hauser is also the author of *Illegal Aliens* in Chelsea House's THE PEOPLES OF NORTH AMERICA series.

CLAYBORNE CARSON, senior consulting editor of the MILESTONES IN BLACK AMERICAN HISTORY series, is a professor of history at Stanford University. His first book, *In Struggle: SNCC and the Black Awakening of the 1960s* (1981), won the Frederick Jackson Turner Prize of the Organization of American Historians. He is the director of the Martin Luther King, Jr., Papers Project, which will publish 12 volumes of King's writings.

DARLENE CLARK HINE, senior consulting editor of the MILESTONES IN BLACK AMERICAN HISTORY series, is the John A. Hannah Professor of American History at Michigan State University. She is the author of numerous books and articles on black women's history. Her most recent work is the two-volume *Black Women in America: An Historical Encyclopedia* (1993).